LONDON TO BRIGHTON DERAILED

Ed Dearnley

First published in Great Britain by Lulu Press, 2010

Copyright © 2010, Ed Dearnley

ISBN 978-1-4461-6736-6

email: ltbderailed@dearnley.org.uk

Cover images by Alexander Klink (Swiss Rea Tower) and David Iliff (Big Ben).

Ed Dearnley asserts the moral rights to be associated as the author of this work

For my Dad

CONTENTS

Raising Some Steam

This is not a book about trains. Well, it's a little bit about trains, but at no point will it go into lengthy considerations on 4-4-0 configurations, bogey cars, piston bores or any of the kind of stuff beloved of men with anoraks, Thermos flasks and notebooks. Instead it's a guide to staring out of the window on the London to Brighton line.

If you live in or around Brighton you can't really escape the London to Brighton line - it's by far the easiest and quickest way to make your way up to the capital. Unlike the sleepy railways heading east and west along the coast the London to Brighton line constantly thrums with activity, with thousands of commuters using the line every day to travel from their homes by the sea to jobs in the city, and countless day-trippers pouring down to Brighton when the sun shines to enjoy a bit of tacky seaside fun.

Gazing out of the window seems to be a popular habit on the train, with people listening to their iPods, pausing for a rest from their books or just eyeing up their neighbour in the window reflection. This is where the idea for this book began; as a regular window gazer I started to notice bits and bobs of interest by the side of the line, and I was keen to find out what they were. The London to Brighton line is not the Orient Express but it does pass through a frequently stunning landscape alive with a history of colourful characters, with the odd grisly crash and murder chucked in for good measure.

In the footsteps of the morning commuters this book's going from south to north, starting off in the hurly burly of Brighton, tearing its way across the glorious Sussex and Surrey countryside and finally winding through the south London suburbs to Victoria station on the north bank of the Thames.

Terminus

Building a railway line is a pain in the bum. The last major new line laid down in the UK, High Speed 1, cost nearly £6 billion and took roughly 20 years between someone thinking a fast line to the Channel Tunnel was a cracking idea, to trains actually rolling down the completed track. And all of this effort to allow people to get to Paris 40 minutes quicker. The problem is all of those tunnels, bridges, cuttings and mile upon mile of track; it's all just rather inconvenient and expensive. So if you're going to go through all of the stress and hassle of building a railway line you've got to make damn sure that the 'B' that you're linking 'A' to is well worth visiting. In the case of Britain 'A' is usually London; now most people would admit that Paris just might be worth a visit, but what's so great about Brighton?

Well the sea is the obvious attraction but in terms of first impressions the rest of the town can often leave something to be desired. In the 1980s Brighton used to have the unfortunate nickname of Skidrow-on-Sea, with visitors often shocked by rundown buildings, a derelict shopping centre, endless traffic and constant harassment from beggars and street drinkers. Even as it weathered the crippling recessions of the 80s and early 90s though there was still something about the place. This is nicely summed up by a spectacularly offensive quote attributed to the then Dean of Brighton University, who cheerfully suggested, "Brighton is like a tart's face: not immediately attractive, but somewhere you'll want to go back to". After this he was probably removed from the top job, and locked away in a far off academic tower where he was less likely to cause offence to most of his student population.

Even after the relentless poshing up of the last 15 years Brighton still retains a somewhat run down feeling, with many parts of town in serious need of some TLC. But judging by the popularity of the place many people turn a blind eye to this and have the same warm feelings towards the town that the Dean was struggling to express. Its popularity is perhaps most evident round the railway station, with an almost constant bustle of commuters, students, foreign day trippers and drunken Londoners depending on what time of day you pass by. Around the station then Brighton feels like a real destination rather than just another stop on the line. There's a reason for this: it is.

Brighton is now widely known as London-by-the-Sea, although looking at the average resident these days Clapham-by-the-Sea is perhaps more appropriate. Even though many Brighton residents sneer at the idea of the town being some kind of outer London borough there's always been an undoubtedly strong link between London and Brighton, a link almost entirely forged by the railway. Even the most ignorant student of Brighton's history will know that the town first became a fashionable resort after the Prince Regent took up residence in the town during the 18th Century, constructing the Royal Pavilion to give himself an impressively bonkers place to live. The Prince was the son of George III who famously went a bit insane making it easy to see why the Prince, also called George, wanted to get a bit of distance between him and his dear Daddy. Initially he moved to Brighton for the professed benefits of sea bathing on his gout, but as time passed he was increasingly attracted to the sex and hedonism that has inspired countless dirty weekends since. Despite the trendy nature of regency Brighton though the town remained rather small, and what really transformed the village known as Brighthelmstone into the resort we know today was the arrival of the railway.

In 1830 Brighton was the most popular seaside destination in the country, attracting about 2,000 visitors a week. Let's put that in context – in a week the most popular seaside resort in the country was attracting roughly the same number of people that can be crammed onto a couple of trains. The reason of course was the long, expensive and uncomfortable journey down from London by horse and carriage. The arrival of the railway in 1841 changed everything, although I'm sure many summer visitors arriving by road will attest that the journey down the A23 is still long, expensive and uncomfortable even though Dobbin has been replaced by an Audi. By 1843 the railway was bringing in over 360,000 people over the summer months and, to serve all of the visitors, the resident population exploded making Brighton the fastest growing town in Britain.

Incidentally a 3rd class ticket in those days would have set you back 3s 6d. That's roughly equivalent to £19 in today's money, rather less than the cost of a peak time return, although these days we do have the benefits of padded seats and a roof. Encouragingly for lovers of progress the journey time from London was initially about 2 hours, over double what it is today, although the bad news is that from the point the line was electrified in the 1930s to today journey times have barely budged.

Arguably the influx of the masses cemented Brighton's success but destroyed its reputation as a fashionable resort for the well to do. Brighton had the last laugh though, and the town's economy has continued to enjoy a mass influx of London day trippers in seek of beer, chips and cheap thrills at the first hint of spring sunshine. In recent years the railway has also generated a significant flow of passengers in the other direction, with thousands of people choosing to live in Brighton and commute to their jobs is the city. Many cite their love of the sea and a more relaxed pace of life for making the commute worthwhile, with weekends by the sea counterbalancing the daily scramble to get a seat on the 18:42 from London Bridge.

Commuters also have the joy of a Grade 1 listed railway station to depart from. When the railways declined in Britain after the Second World War many towns of Brighton's size seemed to be left with positively depressing train stations; perhaps two windy platforms, a damp waiting room and toilets with an eye watering blue light designed to stop junkies shooting up (you have to ask why junkies come to shoot up in train stations, maybe train-spotters keep smack in their Thermoses). Often accompanied by disused sidings and a nice bit of waste land stations can offer a dismal welcome to visitors, and to those waiting for the train they seem to whisper, "Good luck mate but you'd be better off driving".

Brighton station, it has to be said, is no St. Pancras but it does have a certain charm all of its own. On the stagger back from the sea front up the Queens Road, the descent from the West Hill above or the tiring climb up from the trendy North Laine below, the station is always hovering on the horizon somewhere ... although it always seems to be a little bit further to get to than you might think. The station itself is surrounded by the usual collection of pubs, convenience stores and fast food joints found outside most urban stations. Usually pubs, restaurants and shops near train stations should be avoided like the plague – at the very least you'll end up with an empty wallet, but more likely you'll end up with a rapidly emptying stomach a few hours later. However in Brighton somehow this rule doesn't seem to apply. Climbing up the hill the Sussex Yeoman serves up exceptional pub food, whilst if you let gravity take you the other way the Prince Albert pours good beers and hosts noisy up and coming bands. Even the nearest pub to the station, the aptly named Grand Central, manages to impress, with its cute little theatre and a hidden roof garden that encourages the thought of just getting the next train (honest dear) on a warm summer's day.

The station's Grade 1 listing places it alongside some of the grandest buildings in the country. From the front it's kind of hard to see why; OK, it's better than most of the functional yet ugly stations you commonly see, but nothing particularly amazing. But when viewed from the hills at the back the station reveals its true size and nature, with the long curve of the platforms blending into the hillside, and the huge glass and steel roof there for all to see. This is kind of hard to appreciate on the run for a train with confused foreign students and malfunctioning ticket barriers to avoid, but easier as an excuse for a drink in one of the pubs overlooking the back of the station.

Heading Londonwards from Brighton you have two choices of trains; the service to Victoria on the north bank of the Thames, or the cross London Thameslink service that takes the original route of the line to London Bridge before clattering painfully slowly through the city and heading out through Hertfordshire and Bedfordshire beyond. Both trains use the same line for the main part of the journey before heading their separate ways shortly after East Croydon. This book's heading to Victoria if only because of the hideously cramped Thameslink trains that we've had to put up with for nearly 20 years, whose seats have been scientifically proven to be 2 inches narrower than the average English bottom.

As the train leaves the station the imposing viaduct carrying the coast line off to Lewes comes into view to the east. The viaduct marches across the London Road almost like a medieval wall giving access to the inner sanctum of the town. You might wonder how the railway builders had managed to build such big structures in a built up area; the simple answer of course was that they didn't have to. An early painting of the viaduct shows the road running through the arches to open fields beyond, underlining how the arrival of the railway led to the explosive growth of Brighton and the building of the endless rows of terraced houses that cover the hills of the inner part of the town.

It wasn't long of course before many of these crowded terraces became fetid slums, leading to waves of slum clearance and redevelopment from the 1930s onwards. The early redevelopment, it has to be said, wasn't that bad, but as the post war era progressed town planners all over the country seemed to lose touch with reality and engaged in a brutalist game of Top Trumps with their peers. Brighton was not immune, and many of the high rise developments that dot the town centre were built on cleared slums in the 1960s. Much of the development done in this period was so bad it wasn't long before it had to be done again, the original Churchill Square shopping centre being a prime example. By the end of the 80s this had become a semi derelict dump and was redeveloped into the current temple of consumerism in the late 90s.

By the early 70s the town planners had really moved into top gear and were proposing to demolish half the town to lead us to a glorious high rise, car friendly future. The squares and terraces of regency Hove were earmarked for the wrecking ball, to be replaced with more of those fetching high rises. Visitors would be speeded on their way to admire this concrete vision of the future via a convenient elevated expressway from Preston Circus, which would lead them to a giant town centre car park. Unfortunately this would involve knocking down most of the London Road and the North Laine areas, but this was a small price to pay for progress. Whilst demolishing some of Brighton's most elegant homes and trendiest shopping areas now seems frankly insane much of the town at the time was derelict, rather than the thriving place we know today. This doesn't really forgive the planners though, who seemed to regard the lives of everyday people as some kind of inconvenience within their grand schemes of sweeping concrete.

Sometime in the mid-70s the Council's supply of mind-bending drugs for the planning department's water must have run out, and Brighton was saved from becoming the Cumbernauld of the south. A new era of regeneration and conservation replaced the wrecking ball, and areas formally zoned for demolition were slowly brought back to some kind of splendour. The Regency squares of Hove now form flats for the well-to-do rather than squalid bedsits at imminent risk of falling down, whilst the derelict North Laine has been turned into Brighton's trendiest area to shop, drink and live.

The job isn't finished though, and Brighton is still pockmarked with areas in sore need of some sympathetic redevelopment. This is a bit of an opportunity; with the South Downs forming a green girdle around Brighton and Hove the only real options for developing the twin towns is to build on old sites, rather than green-field expansion. The question is then; will Brightonians of the future consider the buildings of the early 21st century to sit with the Regency squares and Victorian terraces, or with the 60s carbuncles that dot the town centre?

Perhaps the answer lies with the New England Quarter that sits to the east of Brighton station. This is yet another slum clearance project, although in this case quite a long winded one. The site was originally a railway works - believe it or not they used to build railway engines in Brighton - and was surrounded by houses for the railway workers. The housing quickly descended into a slummy state, and once the railway works left in the 60s much of it was knocked down to make way for a tawdry mix of tower blocks, car parks and second hand car dealers. By the 90s the powers that be realised the area was a bit of an eyesore and would make a nice spot to house some of Brighton's burgeoning commuter population. The resulting development of a new supermarket, hotel, offices and hundreds of flats is now pretty much finished, with only the last few blocks to complete.

From the outside the new flats look a bit bland, but undoubtedly better than some of the 60s efforts around Brighton. Inside though first impressions are nice, shiny, spangley and ... small. The last comment seems to be an issue with most modern developments; builders squeeze the room sizes to get as many flats onto a site as possible, then compound the problem by putting in huge numbers of bathrooms. It isn't rare to find new two-bed flats that have three toilets, the designers evidentially basing their sanitation needs on a family of three who're suffering from a particularly bad case of the runs.

The fate of the development will ultimately swing with the view of commuters, the New England area undoubtedly being a handy place to live if you want to catch a train in the morning. Whether the commuters will continue to be willing to pay a premium price for this convenience (even a small flat seems to cost well north of 200 grand) and forego a more traditionally 'Brighton' home is anyone's guess, but at least they'll be well scrubbed with all of those bathrooms. What is certain though is that many parts of the town will be redeveloped in coming years, with areas such as the London Road and the old market due for the wrecking ball once the current fog of recession lifts.

Modern development ceases for a bit though once the train has finally left the station area. Preston Park to the east of the line is Brighton's oldest planned park. It's a big grassy expanse that's useful for a Sunday kick about, and used to host some of Brighton's biggest events such as the annual Pride festival that would have the park's Victorian planners shaking in righteous anger – or possibly anticipation. The 15th Century manor and church lying at the northern end of the park provide a reminder that Brighton's outlying neighbourhoods of Preston and

Patcham are actually old villages that the town swallowed up during its remorseless expansion. Preston Park's smaller neighbour is the cute Rock Gardens tucked away between the railway and the London Road, a little treasure trove of water features, bushes and nooks and crannies ideal for whiling away a few hours on a lazy weekend.

Preston Park station itself seems to have been named by a clairvoyant: it was built well before the park opened in 1884. Apparently the 'Park' was added to stop people getting confused between Preston (Brighton) and Preston (Lancashire), which to most of us would be a difficult mistake to make, but then again when you look at the state of some day-trippers returning home you never know. The primary purpose of the station seems to be to frustrate people coming into Brighton – another bloody stop this time less than 2 miles from journey's end, couldn't people just walk? It also makes the area a bit of a commuter oasis for those who find the hurly burly of town centre just a bit too much.

After the station the modern world seems to return to railway line, with innumerable modern flats dotting the space between the train and the London Road. Through the trees to the west you can spy the Withdean stadium, this being the semi-permanent home of the mighty Brighton and Hove Albion football club, known as The Seagulls. They're not mighty of course, they're a bit rubbish, but at least they're interesting with a chequered history and a league placing like some kind of demented yo-yo. The club haven't always been rubbish; they played in the old first division between 1979 and 1983, and almost won the FA cup in 1983. From there though things went rapidly downhill, and they narrowly avoided being ejected from league football in the mid-1990s.

The real blow to the club though came in 1997 when their old ground in Hove was sold off by a somewhat shady majority shareholder to become the site of a Toys 'R Us and several other bland chain stores.

After enduring two seasons of playing 'home' games in Kent the club were given temporary residence at the Withdean, a converted athletics track. An athletics track is of course hopeless as a football ground, but at least Withdean has the minor consolation of situating the away fans about 3 miles from the pitch where their chants of 'we can see you holding hands', 'does your boyfriend know you're here' and 'stand up, cause you can't sit down' can barely be heard. Yes you've guessed it; most visiting fans like to draw attention to Brighton's large gay community rather than aiming their fire at the club's pitiful stadium. The Withdean is also ironically normally full of seagulls, no doubt drawn by plentiful half time burgers and hot dogs rather than the more romantic notion of supporting their namesakes.

Over their stay at the Withdean the club have been involved in a lengthy fight to build a new home. A site was identified next to Brighton's universities near the suburb of Falmer, but considerable opposition was given to the planning application due to its greenfield site. Permission was granted in 2004 and then painfully snatched away due to a legal technicality. In late 2008 though work finally started on the new stadium, with funding secured from a new majority shareholder, Tony Bloom. Know to some as 'The Lizard', Bloom made his money in property, finance and internet gambling as well as making a tidy sum on the professional poker playing circuit. As the credit crunch hit it quickly became apparent that the new stadium wouldn't be receiving any funding from Britain's bankrupt banks; at this point

Bloom broke out his chequebook and personally financed the whole project to the tune of £93 million. As a result, whilst new development ground to a halt across Brighton, the white framework of the new stadium rose from the chalk fields near Falmer, and the club are due to kick off their 2011-12 campaign from their hard won new home. With a bit of luck the new stadium will inspire the club to become the side that a town of Brighton's size sorely deserves, meaning Bloom will get some of his money back whilst the Withdean can go back to being the sleepy athletics track it was before The Seagulls arrived.

Soon after the stadium the railway enters a short tunnel, shoots under the Brighton bypass, then something really rather wonderful happens. Brighton just ... ends. Most towns peter out, becoming a gradually more widely spaced series of suburbs. Due an almost total ban on development on the South Downs north of the Brighton bypass, the town goes from built up urban streets to open countryside in almost the time it takes to cross the road. This means Brighton residents really can get away from it all remarkably quickly, with a short walk, bike ride or drive being all it takes to enjoy the scenic loveliness that is the South Downs.

Easy access to the countryside is one reason why Brighton is a popular place to live. Lots of people think that Brighton genuinely rocks, with thousands of students and twenty-somethings in particular flocking to the town every year. The reasons why people want to live in Brighton are many and varied - for me it's probably the lure of the South Downs on a sunny day, the pier set against the sunset on a bike ride down Madeira Drive and the endless welcoming backstreet boozers. Others though think rather differently, and their reasons for loving the town are things like the music scene, the quirky independent shops or the beach on a hot summer's day.

Brighton is also perhaps something of a Peter Pan town, and sometimes the resident population seems to consist entirely of twenty and thirty-somethings refusing to take the usual post university path of getting a career, settling down and procreating. Brighton's big providers of twenty-something jobs, such as American Express and Legal and General, host innumerable wannabe DJs, bands, writers and .com entrepreneurs, all dreaming of striking it big as they start another year in the low wage job that allows ample opportunity to pursue their main goals in life. The unfortunate truth though is that Brighton's not the best place to make it big – that's the city sitting 52 miles up the train line. Brighton is a good place to talk about starting a revolutionary new business or becoming famous, but London's the place where you need to go to actually achieve your dreams.

Is this a bad thing though? The balding guitarist who refuses to give up on his dream of rock god success can be irritating in his inability to see that the world needs lots of accountants but very few rock stars. But at the same time these people give Brighton a bit of vitality, and dare I say it friendliness, that's missing in towns where everyone's focused on paying the mortgage and getting the kids to school. For the silent majority who've realised that their guitar playing ability is dubious and song writing just plain bad, the dreamers create a relaxed vibe and music culture to enjoy, even if us wage slaves do have to keep one eye on holding down the day job.

CHALK DUST

Right, time for a geology lesson. Sorry I know rocks are rather boring, but here we go anyway. The route covered by the London to Brighton line runs over a geological feature known as an anticline. Here, instead of lying horizontally, the layers of rock beneath the ground have been pushed up in a dome, a bit like your gym honed stomach after a big meal and a few drinks. Over time the dome has been weathered down flat(ish) exposing the successive layers of rock. The outlying areas of the anticline have the original top chalk layer, which now forms the North and South Downs. The area between the two sets of Downs is known as the Weald, with the flat clay areas around Hassocks and Gatwick Airport known as the Low Weald and the hillier central area made of older sandstone rocks and called, unexpectedly, the High Weald.

The practical upshot of all this is that the route from London to Brighton is unrelentingly hilly, and anyone who has ridden the London to Brighton bike ride can tell you that the roads rise and fall like a leg sapping rollercoaster. Until relatively recent times this wild terrain meant Sussex was a pretty backwards place that was largely cut off from the capital, hard to imagine in these days of railways and motorways.

Of course trains throw a wobbly at the slightest sign of a hill to climb, which meant hard choices needed to be made when routing the railway. The London, Brighton and South Coast Railway Company eventually whittled it down to two potential routes, one meandering round Surrey and Sussex like a drunken sailor to avoid steep gradients, with the other taking a more direct route but needing far more in the way of tunnels to be bored and cuttings to be dug. I like to think that the railway company consulted the same psychic who named Preston Park station, concluded that they could piss off annoying 21st century mobile phone chatterboxes with some nice tunnels and settled for the latter route. Happily for us this means the route runs pretty much straight as an arrow all the way to south London, minimising the journey times. This won't have always been the case though; whilst a modern train makes short work of the gradients that this route entailed the first trains had the horsepower of an asthmatic shrew, and the journey times must have been barely better than they would have been on the longer, flatter route.

For a relatively short railway then the London to Brighton line involves some pretty serious civil engineering, with three major tunnels (plus a handful of shorter ones) and a long viaduct thrown over the Ouse valley just north of Haywards Heath. Despite this the railway only took just over three years to build at a cost of £2,634,000 (that's about £265 million in today's money). Compare that to the £5.5 billion earmarked for the increasingly inaccurately named Thameslink 2000 programme to expand capacity on the current cross London route and the original railway starts to look like unbelievable value for money. I guess though that the Victorian railway builders didn't have to worry too much about knocking down people's houses, and with a few friendly palms greased in the House of Lords you probably didn't need to worry too much about planning either.

The railway company worried that the long, dark tunnels might spook the proles in the open roofed 3rd class carriages and hatched a fairly madcap plan to make the tunnels nice 'n friendly by whitewashing the walls and installing gas lighting. Of course gas lit whitewashed tunnels are not really compatible with dirty, fast moving steam trains, and the gas lighting was regularly blown out (a bit dangerous with cinder spitting steam trains around) whilst the white walls quickly became blackened with smoke. Perhaps the railway company could have instead just binned the lights, introduced a few light up Frankensteins (that book was published just in time during 1831) and employed a few spotty youths to jump out of alcoves and grab people's arms.

Unfortunately the above shoddy ghost train gag fits all too well with the history of the Clayton Tunnel under the South Downs. The tunnel is the second longest on the line, boring through the Sussex chalk for over a mile, and in 1861 was the site of what was at the time the worst railway disaster in UK history. Like most railway tragedies the cause of this one was an almighty signalling cock up. Two trains had left Brighton close together and the signal man at the Hassocks end of the tunnel flagged 'all clear' after the first one left the tunnel, unaware that the second train had stopped inside. A third train was flagged into the tunnel and smashed at full pelt into the doomed train inside. The steam locomotive of the moving train obliterated the guards van at the rear of the stationary one before mounting the rearmost passenger carriage and crushing itself against the roof of the tunnel. In all not a good situation for the passengers at the back of the train; their carriage was smashed to bits and a stricken steam engine was stuck above them, pouring flaming coals and boiling water down onto the survivors of the initial impact. The figures reflect the horrific nature of the situation: 23 people were killed and 176 injured.

Thank God for the tunnel though, as boring through the chalk here saved the need to smash any ugly cuttings through the glorious South Downs. People can walk, ride and glide amongst the green hills unaware of the trains speeding deep within the earth below them, or the grizzly history of the tunnel itself.

The South Downs are of course a veritable play-park for outdoor activities in the crowded South East. They stretch across a map of Southern England like a smudge of green ink, rising near Winchester in Hampshire and plunging dramatically into the sea at the Severn Sisters near Eastbourne. It's hard to know where to start on the Downs – libraries of books have been written about their history, scenery and leisure opportunities. Suffice to say though that on a warm summer's Sunday there's very few better places to be than sitting on a hillside, licking an ice cream and watching 101 games of cricket play out in the flatlands of Sussex below.

This is one of the unique beauties of the Downs. Some people say they look dead; after all there are very few trees and hardly any villages on the Downs of any note, just wave after wave of green hills. But this misses the point. From almost every vantage point there's something interesting in the distance to let you know you're in a populated rather than monotonous landscape – the terraces of Brighton, the chalk works near Lewes, and hundreds of tempting pubs in the villages nestling in the lea of the hills.

There's also lots of hidden memories of the past secreted around the nooks and crannies of the Downs, one of the most notable being the Chattri war memorial that clings to the side of the hills to the east of the railway. In the First World War wounded Indian troops were brought to hospitals in Brighton, including one established in the Royal Pavilion, and those who died were cremated at the spot now marked by the Chattri. I first found my way up to the Chattri on a dismal winter's day whilst procrastinating on a university assignment. It's a fine memorial, but it struck me with a sense of great sadness - young men of my age dying horribly in a largely pointless war, with their final resting place being a profoundly alien landscape compared to the far off home that they would never see again.

The Chattri sits on a glorious spot, with a stunning view over the hills into Brighton and the sea beyond. Three concrete pads now mark the spots where the funeral pyres burnt, and are often festooned with flowers and wreaths. It can be an oddly quiet spot; maybe most Brightonians don't know it's there, or perhaps the long uphill slog from the road puts people off visiting. On a sunny day though it's a good place to stop for a rest and ponder the stupidity of war before pushing on to Ditchling Beacon and its tempting ice cream van beyond.

****

The big development for the South Downs is National Park status, which came into effect in early 2010. This is about time too; the South Downs were eyed up when the idea of national parks was first put forward by the Hobnob (sorry, Hobhouse) committee of 1947. Most of the other areas identified by the committee have become National Parks since, but the South Downs have taken over 60 years to get this lofty status. The original refusal was apparently due to the creeping replacement of sheep grazing by the plough on the hillsides, though one would have thought that this would be a reason to raise the level of protection rather than drop it. Munching sheep give the Downs their close cropped grass amongst which dizzying arrays of wild-flowers thrive. If the sheep go the grasslands quickly scrub up and trees move in.

Whilst the park decision was met with wide acclaim it's worth thinking about what the National Park will actually mean. On the face of things it'll see more money for conservation activities, and planning powers within the boundary will be taken away from local councils and given to the new National Park authority. More money must be a good thing, although you might worry that it'll lead to an army of interfering busybodies telling people where they can't ramble, ride or park their paraglider. The planning powers may be a double edged sword; whilst they'll undoubtedly mean that the landscape receives greater protection from obtrusive development, they mean that planning power moves from a democratically accountable Council to an unelected quango. Maybe this is a pessimistic view though, and perhaps this will mean that politicians will no longer be able to pass dodgy developments for electoral gain.

As the train exits the South Downs it's seemingly waved good-bye by two windmills perched up on the hill to the east of the line. Known locally as Jack and Jill the two mills have been around since 1866 and 1821 respectively, although there have been mills on the site for a good deal longer. Surprisingly Jill still works, and occasionally mills out some flour to supply the good people of Sussex for whom normal organic bread just simply isn't right on enough. I should caveat that last statement there; Jill still works thanks to the painstaking work of a group of volunteers who restored the mill and maintain it today. The mills are open to visitors on summer Sundays, and it's well worth the steep climb up from Hassocks station to have a poke around and a cup of tea.

Windmills are relatively common around Sussex. There's at least five still up and in good nick within a few miles of Jack and Jill at Clayton, and they seem to be fondly regarded by the neighbours (Rottingdean use theirs as the symbol of their village). There's a certain irony here that as we enter a new age of wind power National Park status almost certainly means that Jack and Jill won't be joined by any of their modern electricity generating descendants. Whilst few would want to see miles of wind turbines lining the ridge of the Downs I'd think that a few stuck up on the hills overlooking Brighton would look rather elegant, and judging by the bent over trees up there they'd generate a few watts of electricity to boot. Alternatively maybe some enterprising soul could hook Jack up to the grid and get him turning again.

SEX AND THE SLUMBERLAND

As the train shoots out of the end of the Clayton Tunnel you might catch a glimpse of something that looks like a little castle, perhaps thinking that it's some kind of Norman monument. It's not, it's the entrance to the tunnel, built with turrets, fortified walls and arrow slit windows. The Victorians liked this kind of thing, pointless little buildings called follies built to mark some achievement or just because they could be. The castle like building around the entrance to the tunnel falls into the former category: it was built to mark the pretty considerable achievement of building a tunnel through the South Downs.

These days building a tunnel is still a major effort, but we have some pretty nifty kit to help – global positioning systems and lasers to make sure that you're digging in the right place, and tunnel boring machines that look like something out of Thunderbirds. The Victorians didn't have any of this; in fact they had little in the way of machinery and only primitive explosives. What they did have was thousands of men known as navvies; at the height of 19th century railway boom over 250,000 of them were building the railways by day and sleeping next to them by night in hastily built shanty towns. For the Clayton Tunnel alone 6,000 navvies slaved for two years, cutting through the Sussex chalk with their pick axes and blasting powder. When they finished they put up the Clayton folly to end on a high – I bet they also all got pretty drunk too but hell they'd earned it. Modern engineering doesn't really have these nice little finishing touches; the Channel Tunnel for example just has a dull concrete entrance which doesn't really do justice to the immense achievement of those who built it. Maybe things are changing though; recently the go ahead was given for an engagingly bonkers giant horse statue to sit by the side of the new Channel Tunnel railway line near Ebbsfleet.

The Clayton Tunnel folly isn't just purely decorative though, someone actually lives in it. One of the folly's turrets was converted to living accommodation in 1849, but, being a bit cramped, a cottage was built between the turrets to provide more space. Most of us would probably cringe at the idea of an express train whistling past our feet every few minutes, although this wouldn't be the only threat to a good night's sleep: the cottage is also said to be haunted. On the up side the cottage has a nice view, and the nearby Jack and Jill pub is a pleasant enough place to wile away an hour or two.

Shortly after the tunnel the train rolls into Hassocks, a place that didn't even exist before the arrival of the railway and wasn't even formalised as a proper village before 2000. A hassock, I believe, is one of those cushions you're meant to kneel on in church, but how this relates to the name of a train station the almighty one only knows. The story goes that the nearby parishes of Clayton and Keymer couldn't decide what to call the station, ending in a 'Keymer is best!', 'No,

Clayton is best!' playground style deadlock. In the meantime the railway company got bored, picked a couple of names out of a hat and called the station Hassocks Gate. The 'Gate' was presumably a Victorian equivalent of the 'Parkway' name we now give to stations built in the middle of nowhere, and got dropped when the village was built up around the station thus making it in the middle of somewhere.

A better name for the station would have been Hurstpierpoint, the village adjoining Hassocks to the west, although this would have meant a slightly longer, and therefore expensive, sign. Hurstpierpoint has a bit of history to it, being named after the Frenchy sounding Pierpoint family who arrived in 1066 with William the Conqueror. The village centre itself therefore pre-dates the railway, making it a welcome change to the rather soulless commuter towns that seem to dot this area of Sussex.

Just to the south of Hurstpierpoint lies Danny House, an Elizabethan manor house famous for being the place where the song 'Danny Boy' was written in 1910. Actually that last bit's a lie; Danny House's real fame stems from the 6 months that it was rented to Prime Minster David Lloyd-George as his country retreat during the dying days of the First World War. The war cabinet met at Danny House to knock up the details of the armistice with Germany, perhaps an early example of reverse commuting. They must have liked it in Sussex as it seems they didn't want to leave and instead handed the terms over to the Yanks to deliver to the Germans, these being the days when we could hold our heads up to the Americans as equals rather than being told to go and make the tea.

These days Danny House has been converted into retirement flats where randy old men can dream about emulating the achievements of Lloyd-George, who lived in the house with both his wife and his mistress, the distraction probably prolonging the war by at least 3 months. His interesting living arrangements probably explain why he chose to take up residence in rural Sussex, the press in those more gentile times being less likely to make the trip down to Sussex to dig the dirt on the PM's unconventional lifestyle. This was of course a missed opportunity for some marvellous tabloid headlines; perhaps they could have used a highbrow 'Lloyd-George Brokers Tripartite Agreement', or a just plain smutty 'Lloyd-George Opens Up the Big Gun On Two Fronts'.

Whilst Lloyd-George was busy mulling over how many pounds of flesh to extract from defeated Germany another notable figure of the period was hard at work over on the other side of railway. This was artist Eric Gill, who lived in the pretty village of Ditchling between 1913 and 1924. Gill was loosely associated with the Arts and Craft Movement led by figures such as the writer John Ruskin and the multi-talented William Morris. The movement was in part a reaction to the mass production of the Victorian era, and romanticised the attention that traditional craftspeople gave to the production of everyday objects. It's an easy movement to like, incorporating care, attention and art into buildings and objects used every day, rather than being art produced for art's sake. Ironically the movement became a victim of its own success during the Second World War when the cheap utility furniture produced during the period was patterned after Arts and Crafts designs. This led to real Arts and Crafts furniture becoming desperately untrendy, and most of it ended up in skips causing a real headache for those restoring houses hailing from the Arts and Crafts period in more modern times.

Sussex has always been a popular refuge for artists and free thinkers, particularly since the arrival of the railways, due to its fine countryside and close-but-not-too-close proximity to London. Probably the most famous of the lot were the Bloomsbury Group who set up a country home in Charleston Farmhouse to the east of Lewes in 1916. Bloomsbury were an influential group of the time, with their diverse interests covering art, literature and economics as well as a veritable smorgasbord of social thinking. The farmhouse quickly became a refuge for an ever changing circle of artists, and some of their work is still available to see at Charleston and incorporated into the decorations of the nearby church in Berwick. One of Charleston's more famous residents was the novelist Virginia Woolf, who rather dramatically filled her pockets with stones and drowned herself in the River Ooze near Lewes in 1941.

Anyway, back to Gill. Born in Brighton in 1882 he moved to Ditchling in 1913 after a stint in London, followed by his family and a gaggle of attendant artist followers. Ditchling therefore took off as an artist's colony, a real contrast to the pretty but somewhat straight laced place it is today. Gill was active and influential across a number of fields including sculpture, stonemasonry and typeface designing. The latter seems a little odd, but thinking about it most of those fonts in your PC's drop down box pre-date Microsoft Word and were designed by a talented typeface designer at some point. Gill's creations include the eponymous Gill Sans, and Perpetua.

Gill's achievements in arts and crafts are impressive and widely renowned, although in recent years they've been rather overshadowed by his sex life, the seedier details emerging when his diaries were dug up a few years ago. Apparently Gill used to wear a loose fitting cassock to allow himself to whip out little Eric more easily, although it has to be said that I did read that on a religious website where the author wouldn't even type the word penis, instead writing it like this - p****. One hopes that author never suffers a trouser related trip to A&E, as explaining what was wrong might be difficult if he couldn't say what was stuck in his zipper. More reliable though is the knowledge that Gill's sexual appetites unfortunately extended to his daughters and bizarrely his dog, both of which crossed the boundaries of even the relaxed approach to traditional morality held by many artists of the time. Ultimately Gill's loose morals precipitated his exit from Ditchling in 1924, although some of the work of the Guild of Saint Joseph and Saint Dominic that Gill and his followers founded can still be seen in the Ditchling museum.

Whilst Gill wasn't a man you'd want to leave Fido with whilst you nipped away for a few days he was at least colourful, unlike most of the commuter towns that the railway heads for next. In these towns most residents are focused on the more pressing needs of life, with diaries that would perhaps read 'Got up at 5:30, went to work on the train, sealed the big deal, came home, walked the dog'. Gill's would have probably read 'Got up late, created major work of art ...', and I'll leave you to fill in the rest. Most of these towns barely existed before the railway arrived, with a direct connection to London and Brighton being almost their entire reason for being.

The first of these is Burgess Hill which does at least have a prettyish town centre. Wikipedia notes that, 'although a Roman road was built connecting London to the South Coast and passing through what is now Burgess Hill, there is no evidence that the Romans settled', which is presumably because the Romans thought it was boring and would rather live in Brighton. Burgess Hill has two stations, the second one being called Wivelsfield, although it's a bit of a head scratcher as to why as the village of Wivelsfield lies two miles to the east of the station. The station was originally called Keymer Junction, which seems more appropriate as it's here where the line from Lewes meets the London to Brighton main line. It was changed in 1896, I suspect as part of a Southern Railway plot to cut signage costs with shorter station names. The gods evidently didn't like this name change as three years later the station was the site of yet more blood on the tracks when two trains collided in thick fog: six people were killed.

The primitive signalling of the times no doubt contributed to collisions like this one, and when accidents occurred the inherent design of the trains also meant that fatalities were likely – the steam locomotives themselves were full of burning coals and boiling water, whilst the flimsy wooden carriages were notable for offering little protection for passengers and also for smashing into thousands of deadly splinters in the event of a crash. The early history of our railways is therefore marked by some appalling accidents. Happily though modern trains are far more stoutly built with far fewer things on board to blow up and kill people. To prove that point when two modern metal carriaged electric trains collided near Wivelsfield in 1985 (one skidded through a signal) mercifully everybody on board escaped with their lives.

After Burgess Hill the train runs onto its bigger but equally faceless neighbour Haywards Heath. Local legend says the town was named after highwayman Jack Hayward, who used to rob carriages taking rich folk down to the sea, presumably in a drastic attempt to raise enough cash to move somewhere more exciting. Once again Haywards Heath was pretty much non-existent before the arrival of the railway, at which point it boomed in size as commuters moved in. It's a struggle to find anything interesting on Haywards Heath; even the town's website seems to mainly rattle on about the surrounding countryside, before moving on to proudly note that they now have a Cafe Rouge (ohhhhh!) and a Pizza Express (ahhhhh!).

At least the railway gives residents a few options, with the opportunity to sleep soundly in your 3 bed semi then make the odd trip to Brighton or London for an evening out that's a little more vibrant than a trip to Pizza Express. The town is also in spitting distance of the High Weald, a rather nice place for a walk and a pub lunch or, more relevantly here, a quick gallivant through on the train.

HIGH FIVE

The start of the High Weald marks a notable change in scenery from the flatlands around Burgess Hill and Haywards Heath. This area is one of rolling hills covered in woods and hedges, with ancient villages connected by dark sunken roads. In short it's really rather pretty, albeit with a dark and foreboding atmosphere in places.

The entrance to the High Weald for the railway is the viaduct over the Ouse valley, a structure that gets Victorian railway aficionados salivating like Pavlov's dog. The viaduct is a real waymark for the train journey; as the train rolls out of the trees and cuttings and onto the viaduct passengers get a sweeping view for miles up and down the valley. Only the most hardened commuter seems to be able to keep their nose in their book, paper or laptop at this point, and on a good day the carriage looks like a group of mearkats who've just spotted a hungry eagle, with everyone's head popping up to have a good peer out of the window.

With modern mega construction products it's easy to be blasé about Victorian engineering, even something as huge as this viaduct. But like the tunnellers, bridge builders had to work using the primitive materials of the day. For the viaduct over the Ouse valley this meant that the whole structure, 450 meters long and 29 meters high, was constructed using hand laid bricks. The resulting structure is dizzyingly beautiful, a piece of engineering that's also a work of art, actually adding rather than detracting from the wonderful scenery around it. The viaduct is a fitting centrepiece for a Sunday stroll; make sure you go and have a look underneath the arches as well as admiring it from afar, as staring through the 37 hollowed out piers seems like looking into a crazy red brick hall of mirrors. Take a deep breath whilst you're there and check for a faint whiff of tulips as the bricks, all 11 million of them, were shipped in from Holland.

As the train trundles over the viaduct you can glimpse the village of Ardingly to the east, which is the first of the pretty High Weald villages that make a refreshing change to the rather tedious commuter towns further south. Whilst I'm sure it's still stuffed full of outsiders (country term for anyone who can't prove they've lived in the village for at least five generations) the village is exquisitely pretty, and has a nice pub for a pint and Sunday lunch. The view of the village from the train is dominated by the imposing Ardingly College, another product of the Victorian age. Whilst most people appreciate Victorian buildings these days you do have to wonder what the locals thought when a huge viaduct and grandiose private school were dropped in near their little village in quick succession. Similar developments in modern times would no doubt lead to letters to the paper and much frothing at the mouth.

To the modern eye though the Victorian developments add to the character of the village rather than detract from it, as does a more recent development in the form of the Ardingly reservoir. From the train this lies frustratingly out of view, blocked by the hillside. From the air the reservoir forms a V-shape that, if you squint a bit, looks like a stag's head or, if we're being less charitable, like someone flicking a rude gesture to the world. The latter is probably appropriate - it's surprising that the reservoir ever got planning permission as it's younger than it looks, and was only finished off and filled in 1978. It carries off its relative youth due to its small size and the relatively narrow 'arms' of the V shape that in some places make it look more like a river than a reservoir, indeed the roads and nearby houses seems to sweep around the reservoir as though it's been there for generations. This is in real contrast to some of the other reservoirs built around the time, ones further north like Kielder and Rutland Water are all mega-dams, drowned villages and big new roads.

The South East is the driest and most populated part of our country, and water scarcity is a pressing issue. Although fixing leaks and water conservation are part of the solution it's looking like we'll need more reservoirs to cope with the demand, however these are rarely popular and meet with considerable resistance at the planning stage. The Government's solution is the production of a series of National Policy Statements for major infrastructure needs such as reservoirs, railways and big roads, with these guiding the planning decisions of local Councils, rather than the feelings of local residents. Whilst this system has more than a whiff of Bolshevism it should mean that important projects actually get built rather than mired in endless planning battles, but you can only hope that the resulting finished projects are as sympathetic as the Ardingly reservoir.

The next village the train rolls into is Balcombe, another old village with a long history and this time with a train station. Like Ardingly, Balcombe is rather pretty, and the Half Moon pub in the village centre does reasonable food and a mean pint of Harveys, even if the locals and their copious dogs are slightly starey. Balcombe is the kind of place where you can imagine commuting makes real sense – you get to enjoy scenic village life, with a quick train journey up to the Smoke to go to work. A glance at housing costs though reveals that to enjoy this kind of life you'd need a good few zeros on your pay cheque.

Of course one thing commuters know about is trains, and at this point let's turn to the trains that actually ply the line. I'll keep it brief. The first trains running on the London to Brighton line were obviously of the steam variety, in fact near Balcombe you can experience what steam trains would have been like with a ride on the exquisitely named Bluebell Railway. This is part of the old Lewes to East Grinstead line; it was reopened in the 1960s and is now probably the most well-known steam railway in the country, offering a regular service to hordes of tourists every year. Whilst a ride on a steam railway is a nice Sunday afternoon experience, transposing this to the passenger experience of many moons ago leads me to think that steam trains were in fact ... rubbish. They're slow, jerky, have bouncy carriages and suffer from the aforementioned tendency to kill you through steam, hot coals and splinters in the event of an accident. Also from personal experience I can tell you that if you stick your head out of the window of a steam train you tend to get a cinder in your eye.

Three cheers then for the electrification of the line that took place in the 1930s, which led to a blander but more comfortable passenger experience. Electric trains have a lot of advantages over steam or even diesel power; they're quiet, comfortable, efficient, easier to maintain and the trains have no need to return to base for refuelling. The best way of electrifying a line is to put in overhead cables; as the cables are a long way off the ground the voltage can be upped to hair raising levels (this, apparently, being an all-round good thing) and the system sits clear of ground clutter. Overhead cables are expensive though; the cables and their pylons cost a packet, plus bridges and tunnels often need to be modified to squeeze the system in. In the 1930s war weary Britain just didn't have the cash, and across the South East rail lines were electrified with a third rail system that sits alongside the two that the train actually runs along. Compared to overhead cables this suffers from a number of disadvantages, not least that if some poor soul steps on the wrong line they tend to get electrocuted. A more irritating downside for regular travellers is the fact that the third rail sits right down on the ground where it can get covered by leaves, ice and snow. If that happens the train can't get any power and quickly grinds to a halt.

The Thameslink trains, one of the three services running on the line, can run on both the third rail system and the overhead cables north of London, in fact watching the electric pick-ups pop up from the roof of the train is about the most exciting thing about a long wait for a train at Farringdon. These trains were designed before rail privatisation in the mid-90s – before train companies needed marketing departments and catchy names – and they're called 'Class 319s'. They also come from a time where the main design brief was 'make it cheap' and unfortunately it shows. The interior design team seem to have got inches and centimetres confused when looking at the dimensions of the average passenger, or more likely their primary ethos was to crowd as many people into a carriage at the least possible cost. As a result on the busier trains (if you can get a seat) you often find yourself uncomfortably wedged between two other passengers with your knee stuck in the crotch of the person opposite. Luckily these nasty trains are in the process of getting the chop as part of the Thameslink upgrade - perhaps First Capital Connect can run a competition where first prize is to give the lads a hand down at the train scrapyard, as I'm sure they'd have plenty of entrants.

Southern Trains run services into London Victoria and have a fleet of newer, flashier trains. As a result they charge you slightly more than the Thameslink service, meaning that the London to Brighton line is one of the few rail lines where there is real competition for passengers, one of the supposed benefits of rail privatisation. These trains are a product of the marketing age and are called 'Electrostars'; you can tell this when the overhead signs suffer one of their frequent technical hiccups and they say 'Electrostar'. These are good trains; they're quiet, fast and air conditioned, although they perhaps aren't wearing that well. The toilets in particular seem to break all the time, apparently because they're based on aircraft designs and people need to go a lot more on the trains. This is a bit of a head scratcher, as in most people's experience the low pressure on a plane sends you running for the bog, whilst the toilets on trains are normally permanently full of people dodging the ticket inspectors rather than using the facilities.

Before the Electrostars arrived old slam door trains plied the line for nearly 40 years. They might have been a bit old and rattly but they still have a lot of fans - like a 4x4 car you felt you were riding high up on big comfy (chewing gum encrusted) seats. You could also open the door and jump on and off whilst the train was moving, which earned plenty of seasoned commuters a bollocking from the guard. These trains were emblematic of London for a generation; no TV programme on London seemed to be complete without a shot of a train pulling into a London terminal, doors flying open as it juddered to a halt and hordes of smartly dressed city types jumping out. You can't jump from a moving train now though due to electric doors, and at Victoria there always seem to be an eternal wait before you can get out. Apparently this is because the train's on-board systems are unable to get a satellite navigation fix in Victoria station, and the guard needs to amble over to his control panel to unlock the doors.

The slam door trains also had the old fashioned separate compartments for 1st class passengers. These were beloved of some of my compatriots at University who used them to smoke large quantities of weed on the journey up to London, something I always now associate with 'going 1st class'. Smoking a crafty joint is obviously now much harder on trains without the separate compartments, opening windows and slam doors. Other activities are also more difficult, for example a spot of in motion adultery or murdering a man and throwing the body out into a tunnel where, hopefully, he won't be discovered.

OK, so this latter activity wasn't exactly a common occurrence on the railway, but as the train whizzes into the Balcombe tunnel spare a though for poor Frederick Gold who suffered precisely this fate in 1881. Gold's murderer was Percy Lefroy Mapleton, a 21 year old fantasist who doesn't rank as one of history's brightest criminals. The first hint of the trouble in the tunnel came at Preston Park station, which would have given Mapleton up to an hour to come up with a cunning way to get away with his dastardly crime. Instead he staggered out of his carriage at Preston Park covered in blood, and told the station master that he'd been attacked and knocked out by two men. However, it was at this early stage that his story started to unravel; the guard noticed that he had a gold chain sticking out of his shoe, surely something his attackers would have relived him of.

Given the benefit of the doubt Mapleton was taken to Brighton police station where he gave a statement and offered a reward to find his attackers. He then went on to the hospital, where the next sign appeared that something was not quite right with his story. Mapleton was covered in blood yet his wounds were fairly superficial, so where the hell had all the blood come from? Despite these suspicions, and also a search of his clothes which turned up some antique medals that he claimed to know nothing about, Mapleton was allowed to leave for a relative's house in Surrey, albeit with a police escort. Meanwhile a search of the railway carriage in which he was allegedly attacked turned up three bullet holes and blood splattered left, right and centre.

Finally a search of the line was organised, and in the Balcombe tunnel the grisly discovery of Frederick Gold's body was made. He'd been shot, stabbed and robbed of his cash and valuables. Luckily for Gold's dignity he'd landed between the tracks, so he wasn't hit by any passing trains, not that this mattered to his general health as he was stony cold dead. Nearby a bloody knife was found, but remember this was before the days of fingerprints and modern forensic science, although in this case the question of 'who done it?' would not be taxing many brain cells. A telegram was sent up the line to Three Bridges and the detective accompanying Mapleton was told not to let him out of his sight. Cunningly though Mapleton gave him the slip. On arrival at the relative's house Mapleton asked the detective to wait outside whilst he changed his clothes; the detective agreed, seemingly unaware that a man under suspicion of murder might just jump over the back fence and do a runner.

The ensuing manhunt was notable for the sensation it caused in Victorian Britain, and also for being the first time an artist's impression of the perp was used in a 'wanted' picture; the drawing was also published in the Daily Telegraph. The picture is curiously bad, making Mapleton look like some shark faced nut in a bowler hat, and the practical upshot was that false sightings poured in from up and down the country. Fortunately for the police the true location of the master criminal's lair was found within a few days, when Mapleton helpfully sent a telegram to his employer asking for his wages to be forwarded to his new address ('Dear Boss, sorry I haven't been in for a while, I had a killer weekend in Brighton. Could you please forward my wages to The Evil Murder's Lair, 44 Vine Street, London. Yours, Percy'). On arrival the police found that he'd also failed to get rid of his bloody clothes, giving them some nice evidence to use at the subsequent trial.

As the trial approached the media storm around the case intensified, and Mapleton and Gold even had their own waxworks in Madam Tussauds for a while – no doubt in the Chamber of Horrors, or possibly the Cellar of Idiots. At his trial Mapleton decided to wear full evening dress to impress the ladies and gentlemen of the jury, however it didn't do him much good. The evidence against him was such that it only took 10 minutes for the jury to find him guilty, and he was subsequently hung in Lewes prison bringing the whole sorry saga to a close.

The Balcombe Tunnel is also meant to be haunted by three First World War soldiers killed whilst sheltering from a storm inside, although most sightings are probably down to people who've had one too many in the nearby Half Moon and missed the last train home. One would think that a railway tunnel wouldn't be the most sensible place to shelter from the elements, but judging by Percy Lefroy Mapleton common sense was in short supply around the turn of the century.

As the train leaves the tunnel (another whopper incidentally at over 1100 meters long) it starts to leave the High Weald too, and gradually the sight of modern housing estates at the side of the tracks mark a return to the modern world, or more specifically Crawley. Now, Crawley sounds like an unpleasant disease of the downstairs variety ("Alright Steve, yeah I went to a stag party in Budapest and came back with a nasty rash: the doc says it's the Crawlies") and doesn't look too pretty, but it is at least a somewhere town with a strong local economy, indeed many Brightonians commute up to Crawley due to the lacklustre job opportunities in Brighton itself. The origins of the town go back a long way, the name actually derives from the Saxon settlement of Crow's Leah; a crow infested clearing in the woods. When Brighton took off as a seaside resort Crawley began to grow due to its position halfway along the London to Brighton road, making it a convenient place to stop and rest on the journey down to the sea. The coming of the railway sped this process up, and at one point a quarter of the town's population were employed in businesses related to the railways.

Crawley's stop on the line is called Three Bridges, with Crawley station proper sat one stop down on the line to Horsham. God knows what bridges the name refers to, the railway doesn't go over too many, but originally Three Bridges was a little hamlet sitting a mile or so from Crawley itself. The New Towns project after the Second World War created the brick and concrete link between the two, with the area as a whole designated for major expansion which in effect filled all of the gaps between the old villages.

The New Towns era gave us many of the architectural gems that dot the countryside around the M25 including Bracknell, Stevenage and Hatfield; as with Crawley these towns were in the main built by massively expanding old historic cores. The modern equivalent is of course the previous Government's Eco Towns project, which puts a green gloss on an old formula. At the time of writing most of the proposed Eco Towns seem to be dying a slow death, so it remains to be seen if many other areas of the country will be catching the Crawlies soon.

As it exits Crawley the train waves goodbye to Sussex and hello to Surrey, marking roughly the halfway point of the journey. From here to the North Downs we're back in the environment of commuter towns and major developments, the biggest of the lot growing like a particularly virulent mould just to the north of Crawley.

THE IDIOTS

Gatwick Airport is another place that owes its existence to the train line; situating London's second airport out here in the Surrey countryside only makes sense with a fast rail connection to rush people into the city. As the train leaves Three Bridges it passes through development ringing the airport: light industry, huge office complexes, endless carparks then finally the airport terminal itself. Before pulling into the airport station the railway scrapes the end of the runway, a slightly disturbing experience at times with aircraft swooping low over the roof of the train waking up many a commuter from their peaceful slumber.

Most people would grudgingly admit that Gatwick, or Brighton International as it's known down by the sea, is a pretty good airport as far as they go. Compared to some vast behemoth like Heathrow it's compact with only two terminals linked by a nifty little monorail. Train access is easy with the station built practically under the main terminal rather than the usual 5 miles away. Gatwick's location also gives it advantages. Runways are normally laid east to west, so that aircraft can take off into the prevailing westerly winds that we experience in the

UK, and in Gatwick's case this means that the planes take off and land over the relatively sparsely populated Surrey countryside. Aircraft serving Heathrow on the other hand travel over central London and the Thames valley, meaning that millions of people get to enjoy the noise and air pollution and in the event of an accident we can wave goodbye to, say, Richmond.

The niceties of Gatwick don't hide that it's a busy old place though, the second largest airport in the UK and busiest single runway airport in the world. The latter is either a lamentable failure to invest in capacity or a triumph of British efficiency, depending on your view. Once it had been designated as London's second airport by the Government in the 1950s Gatwick never looked back and blossomed in size, with a second terminal added during the 1980s at a cost of £200 million and constant tinkering to expand the number of planes and passengers you can shovel through ever since.

The obvious question for those who live around the airport is 'what happens next?' - will the airport stop at its current size or continue to expand? The recent development at Gatwick is that it's been sold to the cuddly sounding Global Infrastructure Partners for a wallet crunching £1.5 billion. Historically London's three main airports have all been owned by the British Airports Authority, a former Government owned utility privatised in the 80s and now owned by a Spanish conglomerate. Now, you don't need to be an avid student of economics to realise that the same company owning Gatwick, Stanstead and Heathrow isn't good news for competition, with little incentive to improve costs and services for the long suffering passenger. The Government belatedly recognised this in 2009 and ordered the sale of Gatwick and Stanstead.

Keen to recoup that £1.5 billion outlay Gatwick's new owners have signalled their intentions to build a second runway. These plans might just run into some headwinds though. Firstly the airport is sandwiched tightly between the towns of Crawley and Horley, which limits room for expansion without demolishing bits of northern Crawley and exposing lots more people to low flying planes. A second runway also runs counter to the previous Government's 2003 'Future of Air Transport White Paper' and an agreement between the airport operator and the local council not to build another runway before 2019, although past experience shows these policy decisions can be quickly reversed.

There is of course the question of whether we should be expanding our airports at all, with the negative environmental effects of flying well documented in the mainstream media. The aviation industry claim that without expansion, particularly at Heathrow, the UK will turn into an economic backwater, people will lose their jobs and within no time at all we'll be back in the stone-age, cracking open each other's heads to feast on the sweet goo within. The 'antis' on the other hand claim that the economic argument is overplayed, and that more aircraft will cause lots of noise and air pollution, and pump out more greenhouse gases than several billion flatulent cows.

It's easy to be nonchalant about these downsides, after all most of us don't live near enough to an airport to be affected by the noise and air pollution, and fears of climate change can be eased by the aviation industry's recent announcement that they'll halve greenhouse gas emissions by 2050. Unfortunately under closer inspection these comforts start to fall apart; emissions control seems to be based on blind hope rather than anything the engineering eggheads have under development in the lab, whilst the ballooning number of planes mean that more and more of us will have our skies criss-crossed by low flying aircraft as they rumble round to land at increasingly busy airports.

Taking the green option and limiting aviation expansion is likely to have a simple effect though: flying will become more expensive. This is a bit of a worry, as most of us mutter green platitudes but can't quite resist that cut price European city break. Funnily enough a recent survey suggested that individuals who claim to have the greenest ideals tend to make the most flights, the reason being that they tend to be the most well off. Poorer people spend less time worrying about the environment (they've got keeping the wolf from the door to worry about), but take the greener holiday option of clipping tokens out of the Sun for a £5 caravan holiday in Devon.

The choice then is rather stark; either airports expand and damn the environmental consequences, or we accept that the cheap air era is coming to a close and, for the time being, we won't be able to repeat the hyper air mobility of the past 15 years. Two thoughts might jump into your mind when you think about that, the first (rather non-green) one is that it might be an idea to bag as many countries as you can whilst flying is still cheap. The second is that if Gatwick becomes a bit quieter there might be less chance of getting whacked in the head by a suitcase as zillions of jet-lagged passengers stumble onto the train at the airport station.

Gatwick's northern bookend is Horley, another unremarkable town that was a dot on the map before the arrival of the railway made it a convenient spot for commuting to the capital, and the growing airport provided jobs for those adverse to morning train journeys. Surprisingly Horley has a historical society, surprising as it doesn't have much in the way of history, although they did manage to unearth that Malcolm Campbell spent a few years living in neighbouring Hookwood before the war. Campbell was an early 20th century speed freak – if he was alive now he'd probably be down at Gatwick fitting rockets on the back of a jumbo in a bid to make it into orbit. With his Bluebird series of cars he broke the land speed record nine times, before turning his attention to boats and breaking three water speed records. Smug German saloon car drivers will be pleased to know that Campbell's first land speed record in 1924 was 146 mph - you could probably break that now on the M23, although PC Plod might have something to say if you got caught.

Campbell's greatest achievement is perhaps the fact that he didn't die trapped in the burning wreckage of a car, as the 'grizzly death in a crash problem' afflicted a great many of his compatriots in daring-do of the time. Instead he died of a stroke at his home in Reigate in 1943, one would hope whilst tinkering away in his garage trying to work out how to squeeze a Spitfire engine into a sportscar. Campbell's son Donald took over the family business, building a series of his own Bluebirds to trump his Dad's land and water speed records; unfortunately in 1967 his boat flipped at over 300mph on Coniston Water in the Lake District, dealing him the fate his father managed to avoid.

Both Campbells would probably be hopping mad that the train can do no more than 90mph as it passes through Horley. This looks likely to remain the top speed for the foreseeable future, despite the persistent rumour in Brighton that there's going to be a 35 minute service to London at some point soon (a rumour no doubt stoked by greedy estate agents trying to get a few more Londoners to move down to the coast). This rumour probably stems from the last speed run attempt in 2005 where a Southern train managed to make the trip in just under 37 minutes. This is obviously a bit faster than the current express, but the fact that all the other trains were cleared out of the way and the train didn't stop anywhere means it's not going to be part of the regular service any time soon. In all honesty the line is not really good enough to go much faster anyway, and on some of the bumpier parts of the track they'd be coffee and iPods flying all over the carriage at anything above the current crawl.

After Horley the railway passes into the last bit of open countryside before it plunges into the North Downs and London beyond. Here it does something that an invading German army might have found a little difficult; it crosses a defence ring, a line of fortifications constructed in World War II to protect London. From the train you can see a pillbox in the fields to the east, with another one cunningly hidden from sight and seemingly well placed to lob a few shells at a passing train. In case you're not familiar with pillboxes they're the little World War II concrete bunkers that, these days, are usually filled with piles of empty beer cans and enveloped by a heavy smell of wee. As an island nation it would seem to make sense to build these things on the coast to throw the invaders back into the sea, and to find one here in the Surrey countryside seems quite odd.

Anyway, it turns out that this defence line was built during the invasion fears that followed the fall of France. During the run up to the war the French had built a formidable series of fortifications of their own on their border with Germany, known as the Maginot Line. Rather unsportingly though the Germans refused to attack the line directly and instead nipped through lightly defended Belgium to deliver a hefty kick to the French behind before booting us Brits into the sea at Dunkirk. The British solution to this obvious fault with the French system was to build defensive lines absolutely everywhere, with the sea preventing an invading army from using the 'Belgium tactic'. The line that crosses the railway is part of the grandly named General Headquarters Line that starts in Somerset before wrapping round London and heading up to Yorkshire.

The idea that a thin line of pillboxes and ditches could stop all the planes, tanks and soldiers that the Germans could have thrown at it seems a little hopeful – surely they'd have just flown over the top and dropped paratroopers to attack the line from the rear? Luckily for us we never got to find out, as after putting Britain on the ropes Hitler made the mad decision to attack Russia instead of finishing us off. Whilst the thick concrete walls were never tested by German shells the pillboxes now have a new enemy, Mother Nature, and under constant attack from undergrowth and the weather they're starting to fall apart. Hopefully the roofs of these ones will hold out for a bit though, as with the expanding estates of Horley heading rapidly towards them they'll make an excellent place for bored teenagers to get frazzled on cider.

Just before the train hits Redhill there's a big, impressive, obviously Victorian building to the east of the line (obscured by trees a bit in summer); this is the gloriously named Royal Earlswood Asylum for Idiots. You have to admire the Victorians for calling a spade a spade; if it was built in modern times the asylum would have been given a name that would have you scratching your head for hours before you worked out what it was for. They lent this approach to most of their charitable work and campaigns – a glance at a list of Victorian charities throws up gems such as the Cripples Home for Orphans and the Destitute and the Society for Improved Condition of the Labouring Classes. With the charity sector going through a round of re-branding at the moment maybe we could return to the Victorian naming model. Greenpeace could perhaps be Hands Off Our Whales You Scandinavian Bastards, the Association of British Drivers could become the Society for Angry Middle Aged Men Who Want to Drive Really Fast Without Being Nicked By Speed Cameras, and Scope could go back to being the Spastics Society.

Actually the term spastic is perhaps a good example of how medical terms for those deemed sub normal gradually seep into popular insults, as it used to be a medical term before being picked up as a playground insult in the 1970s. The word idiot also used to be a medical term before being turned into a means of insulting your mates. Apparently the definition of an idiot is a person with a mental age below three years, an imbecile three to seven years, whilst a moron is a person with a mental age of between seven to twelve years. So now you know precisely what you're calling traffic wardens and Dave in accounts, and on past form you'll probably be calling them a Scope in a few years' time.

Anyway, back to the asylum. The grand neo-gothic building opened in 1855, with construction entirely funded by public donations. Queen Victoria herself dug into her well stuffed pockets to the tune of 250 guineas. The first warden (or medical superintendent if we're being polite) was a chap named John Langdon-Down, who first described the condition named after him: Down's Syndrome. Down would have fitted in well with the modern politically correct medical profession, publishing sensitively titled papers such as the 'Observations on the Ethnic Classification of Idiots'. In this paper he tried to link the various types of mental illness with ethnic groups. Down's Syndrome was linked to Mongolians, which explains why people with Downs are sometimes called Mongols by the older generation.

The asylum's most famous, or more correctly most infamous, residents were two sisters named Katherine and Nerissa Bowes-Lyon. If you can't place the names then let me help. Bowes-Lyon was the late Queen Mother's maiden name; the sisters were the Queen's cousins. Both sisters were born with severe mental disabilities and were quietly dumped in the asylum in 1941, with the Royal Family telling the outside world that they were both dead. The sisters never received a visit from a member of their family, who conveniently pretended these 'shameful' members of the royal clan didn't exist, which unfortunately seems to have been quite the norm for the aristocracy of the time. The story caused a major splash when it leaked out in the 80s; it's just a shame the Queen didn't take the opportunity to make amends, as if the royal family acknowledged their less fortunate members it might have put more onus on the care of the mentally disabled in this country and beyond. The fact that both the Queen Mother and the Countess of Wessex have been patrons of the charity Mencap is particularly ironic.

Nerissa died in the asylum in 1986 and was buried in an unmarked pauper's grave before belatedly being given a proper headstone. Katherine was shipped out to a care home later that year when the hospital closed down, and, as no report of her death has ever surfaced, we can assume that she's still living anonymously in a home somewhere in Surrey. So when that old lady tells you she's 3rd in line to the throne next time you visit your Granny she might just be telling the truth. Come to think of it who knows how many other inconvenient members of the royal family are stuffed in care homes around the Home Counties.

The asylum building itself is still a grand old place with amazing detailing and a seemingly endless parade of elaborate carvings, stout pillars and soaring towers knocking the cheapo buildings we put up today into a cocked hat. It takes its place alongside the other great buildings of this age of Victorian philanthropy, another nearby example being the Holloway Asylum in Virginia Water. Holloway was an interesting character; after amassing his fortune by flogging mountains of pills of questionable medical value he kicked off a public debate on 'how best to spend a quarter of a million or more' (that's about £25 million in today's money), eventually blowing the lot on the aforementioned asylum and the even grander Royal Holloway College near Staines.

Both the Holloway and Royal Earlswood asylums have suffered a similar fate. Along with most of the big Victorian mental institutions they were closed down in the 80s, when the policy of care in the community was thought to be a better way of caring for the mentally disabled than locking them up for life. Both asylums have now been converted into gated developments of luxury flats, kind of ironic considering their former occupants, and are now festooned with 'keep out or our private security will shoot you in the head' style signs, which rather limits Jo Public's ability to check out this example of our Victorian heritage. Surrey isn't exactly a high crime area, and you have to ask yourself what kind of people feel they need to live sheltered behind iron gates and private security guards, now keeping people out rather than in. To answer this conundrum we can turn to none other than Victorian king pin Prince Albert, who when opening the asylum on the 5th July 1855 said, "I hereby declare this Asylum to be open for the care and education of the Idiot and Imbecile for all time to come". Note the last five words.

KABLAM!

Redhill town-centre is ugly. Well, I know that's true of many of the towns on the London to Brighton line, but despite its cosy name and idyllic location Redhill town-centre really does take the prize: it's really, really ugly. You can almost imagine the conversation in the Council planning department ...

"Hey, I've got an idea! Let's drive a socking great dual carriageway right through the town centre - drivers will be able to get places 5 nanoseconds quicker whilst those cheapskate pedestrians can suck fumes and spend ages crossing the road"

"Brilliant idea, let's do it!"

"After that let's fill the entire place with a load of big mismatched buildings whose only common thread is their awesome ugliness"

"Magic, this is pure gold!"

"Finally let's put down some really confusing and downright dangerous cycle paths, that way we can turn more drivers into dribbling wrecks when they accidental run someone over and keep the beds warm in that asylum down the road"

"You're a genius; you'll get a knighthood for this one!"

Redhill is perhaps nicely summed up by the treatment of its museum, which houses some interesting bit and bobs from the Royal Earlswood Asylum for Idiots. Booted out of its former home and with the Council too skint to cough up for a new building, the best bits from the museum are now lodged in a couple of display cases in the town's Belfry shopping centre. Shoppers get the opportunity to gawp at the creations of idiot savant James Henry Pullen (which include a rather impressive model of Brunel's Great Eastern steam ship) as they search in vain for the carpark ticket machine, no doubt confused as to why the Redhill branch of Modelworld doesn't appear to have any doors.

In short then Redhill town-centre could do with blowing up, which is rather appropriate as it's where Alfred Nobel first demonstrated dynamite in 1867. Nobel is of course best known these days for the prizes named in his memory, however the money used to establish the prizes came largely from the success of his arms manufacturing businesses. Kind of ironic considering the best known Nobel Prize is the one given for peace.

To be fair to Nobel his best known creation, dynamite, has many peaceful uses in addition to blowing your enemies to merry hell. Prior to dynamite the only real option for the kind of blasting needed in quarrying, construction, tunnelling and what have you was gunpowder, which is far less effective when you need to blast apart a lot of rocks. A much more powerful alternative existed, nitroglycerine, but this liquid explosive is monumentally unstable and has the habit of exploding if you so much as give it a dirty look. An accidental nitroglycerine explosion took the life of Nobel's own brother in 1864, which must have concentrated his mind on finding a safer replacement. Nobel's eureka moment came when he discovered that nitroglycerine could be absorbed into another substance to make it far more stable and easy to handle, yet still retaining much of its explosive grunt. Rolled into a cylinder and wrapped in paper this gives us the familiar stick of dynamite beloved of quarrymen, civil engineers and Wile E. Coyote.

Dynamite has of course also been held dear by warmongers over the 19th and 20th centuries, and Nobel aided and abetted this by establishing several arms companies to churn out guns and bombs; he didn't live to see the arms golden ages of the First and Second World Wars though. The establishment of the prizes that bear his name is thought to stem from a premature obituary in the French press, published in 1888, when the death of Nobel's brother was confused with the big man's own demise. Very few people would want their obituary to start 'the merchant of death is dead', before continuing 'Dr. Alfred Nobel, who became rich by finding ways to kill more people faster than ever before, died yesterday'. A bit of a change to the modern habit of fawningly uncritical obituaries then.

Chastened by this experience Nobel left the majority of his considerable fortune to establishing his prizes. There are five prizes in all, one each for achievements in physics, chemistry, medicine, literature and peace. Whilst the peace prize normally captures the headlines, with high profile winners such as Barack Obama, Al Gore and Nelson Mandela, the other prizes are perhaps even more important, with the award of a Nobel Prize marking the crowning achievements of a truly remarkable career. Since their establishment the Bank of Sweden has funded a sixth prize for economics. This has caused some controversy, and perhaps the recent total economic cock up aided by some of the followers of the so called dismal science will support calls to end winners of the economics prize standing shoulder to shoulder with the great laureates of the traditional sciences.

The Nobel Prizes are now parodied by the similarly named Ig Nobel awards, which as the name suggests is a showcase for less enlightening scientific research that will get a cheap laugh. Recent winners included a demonstration that high-priced fake medicine is more effective than low-priced fake medicine, the ground breaking discovery that professional lap dancers earn higher tips when they are ovulating and twin announcements on the effectiveness of Coca-Cola as a spermicide. In case you're wondering the last one saw a US team claim that Coca-Cola works well as a spermicide, whilst a parallel study from Taiwan pronounced it totally useless. Perhaps a more useful study would be one examining how truly desperate you'd have to be before you started using fizzy drinks for your birth control needs.

Back to Redhill then, and rather than blow it up the powers that be seem to be trying to make it even bigger, with the train line passing development after development as it tracks its way round the edge of town. The biggest of the lot is the rather nicely named Water Colour development, which falls to the east of the line as it passes the top end of Redhill. This development has seemingly been under construction for years now, with 500 homes going up around two scrubby looking lakes although I'm sure it'll look a lot nicer when they actually finish the damn thing. Water Colour's website is naturally rather gushing, with the tag line 'homes that allow you to escape to the country with the town just a heartbeat away' and stressing the marvellous transport links the development enjoys. Whilst this is undoubtedly true, the pretty North Downs are a couple of miles distant, you have to wonder whether people will be so delighted with the fact that the development is sandwiched between a rather large landfill site, a railway line and two busy motorways. The sense of peace might also be upset by the odd plane circling round to land at Gatwick.

But that's probably unfair to Water Colour; they seem to have made an effort to turn it into a bit of a community rather than row upon row of identical commuter hutches, with the developers providing communal gardens, shops and a doctor's surgery. Despite the pretty houses round the lakes though Water Colour seems to mainly consist of block upon block of flats, slightly odd in a development that seems designed for commuters with families. Whilst flats make sense in crowded urban areas like Brighton, where people want to live centrally to train stations and entertainment, it makes very little sense in a development a mile distant from a dullsville like Redhill where people would seem to want a house with a garden and somewhere to park the car.

It turns out that the flats at Water Colour follow a bit of a trend; nationwide the number of family houses being built has fallen whilst the number of flats constructed has sky-rocketed. With a recent realisation that this might not be such a great thing there's a bit of mutual finger pointing as to the reasons behind the trend, with some blaming Government targets that mandated high housing density and pushed development onto small brownfield (previously developed) plots. Others blame demand from buy-to-let investors, who favour 2-bed flats for their lower price and suitability for the twenty-something lettings market. Whoever is to blame, the result is that in many parts of the country there's an oversupply of flats and a serious shortage of family homes. This pushes the price of family homes up and up, and to buy one in Water Colour you won't be looking at much change from 400 grand.

You can kind of see where this all might go; what most people consider to be a 'nice' family house - reasonable size place with three bedrooms, garden and somewhere to park the car - will become the preserve of the better off, whilst the rest of us will have to get used to bringing up our families in small flats, unable to make the jump to a proper house. Maybe we'll escape this future though; one benefit of the recent recession and housing market crash seems to be the Government and house builders reversing their thinking, and boosting the number of proper houses earmarked for construction.

Dodgy housing isn't confined to modern flats though, for example you could live in a Park Home. A site of these sits to the west of the railway line just after Water Colour. Park Homes are the rather nice name given to the British equivalent of trailer parks, with the homes themselves ranging from full on mobile homes to something that looks a bit more substantial. Even the chunkier ones are still mobile though - these are the houses you sometimes see on the back of a massive lorry going up the motorway, you know, the ones where you think you're going to get a drainpipe though the windscreen as you pass in the next lane. Park Homes suffer from a bit of a dodgy reputation with some site owners having a nasty tendency to screw tenants, and the homes themselves being kept way beyond their temporary design life and showing it. They also tend to be stuck in crappy out-of-the-way locations on the edge of town. The ones by the side of the line actually have a pretty good plot closish to the centre of Redhill, although the fact that they're hemmed in between two railway lines is probably the reason why the site hasn't been flogged off to build some slightly more desirable housing.

Speaking of the two railway lines, the London to Brighton line does something a bit funny around Redhill: it splits in two with a sort of Redhill bypass. This may not be immediately apparent, but in the end the suspicious extra tunnel on the bypass line will give the game away. You would have thought this has something to do with some early capacity problems – a train equivalent of motorway widening – but no, it has more in common with two neighbours feuding over a shared path.

The way our railways are now organised is almost incomprehensibly muddled. One company owns all of the tracks, other companies owns the trains that run on the tracks and finally a multitude of other companies actually operate the train services, paying the other companies for use of their trains and tracks. In Victorian times things were a bit simpler; if you wanted to operate a railway company you built the railway, bought some trains and ran the services yourself. As the railways expanded though they began to run into their neighbours, which caused a few problems. The section of line around Redhill is where the London, Brighton and South Coast Railway met the South Eastern Railway, and they were forced by the Government to share the construction and running costs of this part of the line. Soon after the line was built they realised they didn't like sharing at all, and spent the next 60 years falling out and squabbling about it. Eventually the LBSC

Railway stomped off in a huff to build their own line between Redhill and Coulsdon, completing it in 1899.

Building a whole new line is a pretty expensive way to resolve a neighbourly squabble, particularly when it involves blasting two new tunnels. The first one isn't too long – it simply ducks under a hill to the east of Redhill – but the main tunnel through the North Downs is a whopper. The tunnel, along with its near neighbour on the older line, is well over a mile in length, and both lines travel through some seriously long cuttings on the northern side of the tunnels (the longest in Europe apparently) before joining up again in Coulsdon. All-in-all the line cost £85,000 or about £8 million in today's money, which sounds cheap compared to modern transport projects but is a pretty serious price to pay for falling out with your neighbours. In case you're wondering most trains follow the newer line, with the slower services that need to stop at Redhill taking the older one.

Hey, guess what happened in the tunnel? If you've read this far you've probably realised that unpleasant things tend to happen in tunnels, and you'd be absolutely right. In 1905 the body of a Miss Mary Money was found in the tunnel, she'd been murdered, or at least murder was suspected, as unlike Balcombe tunnel dimwit Percy Mapleton this murderer was pretty good at covering his tracks. The signs of foul play were clear; Mary's body had what looked like a gag in her mouth, and when the train emerged from the tunnel it was seen with all of its doors closed, meaning that, barring a freak accident, someone had closed the door after she fell from the train. The suspicion was that Clapham dwelling Mary had met up with a male friend and got on the train for a trip down to Brighton, at which point her friend's plans turned out to have more to do with robbing and murdering her than enjoying a romantic weekend. The full story will never be known though, as after Mary's horribly injured body was found inside the tunnel all trails went cold and her murderer was never apprehended.

The reason for all the tunnels of course is the North Downs, which mark the end of the anticline (remember that?) that the railway has been traversing since Brighton. Superficially the North Downs are a mirror image of their southern counterparts, starting near Farnham in Surrey and running for 120 miles before crashing into the sea in Kent to form the white cliffs of Dover beloved of RAF pilots and Dame Vera Lynne. Like the South Downs before them they are protected by some Areas of Outstanding Natural Beauty designations, and have a nice long distance trail running along their length for multi-day hikes and nutjob cyclists to ride in one day.

The character of the North Downs is rather different from their southern neighbours though; they have more woodland than the bald sweeping vistas down south, and are far more developed with a myriad of towns, villages and roads nestling amongst the hills. However, apart from the unwelcome intrusion of the M25 the villages, roads and even some of the towns add to the character of the hills. Unlike the South Downs you don't have to drop down off the hills to nip into that nice country pub, you can just wander from village to village and enjoy the countryside in between.

Of course the North Down's beauty and proximity to London pulls in day-trippers like a cow pat attracts flies, and on a hot weekend the Downs crawl with people walking, biking, horse riding, paragliding, zorbing and whatever other activities people can dream up to do on the side of a hill. Amongst the busiest areas are Box Hill and Leith Hill, which lie to the west of the line near Dorking. Leith Hill is the highest point in south east England, and has got to be one of my favourite places in the country, if only for the fantastic tower that sits at the top of the hill where you'd normally only expect to find a nice view. The tower was built in 1766 by a chap called Richard Hull, who was a little bit eccentric in the best tradition of English aristocrats. One day – presumably whilst herding his cats through the hills – Hull thought that it was a real shame that Leith Hill was only 965 feet above sea level. Wouldn't it be nice if there was something on the hilltop that would take it above that magic 1,000 foot mark? With that in mind he set out with his bricks and shovel to make it happen, or more likely got someone else to do it for him – you'd imagine he had a quid or two.

Hull died in 1772 and is buried beneath his beloved tower. The story goes that his coffin was placed vertically into the ground with his head facing down, as he thought that on Judgement Day the world would be turned on its head and wanted to arise from his grave the right way up. Amazingly this was confirmed when the tower was last renovated, and Hull still lies in his vertical coffin to this day. What a guy, he should have been given a knighthood and a key role in the House of Lords. After his death the tower fell into disrepair before being restored by the National Trust in the 1980s. Today the tower is open to the public, and on a clear day you can enjoy views into central London before turning round and gazing back to the Channel coast. Of far more interest though is that the National Trust has decided to run a cake shop from the base of the tower where two friendly ladies are usually on hand to dish out ice creams, tea and home-made cakes. This makes the tower a bit of a honeypot for all of those walkers, bikers and zorbers, and on a warm summer's day with a slice of cake in their hands everyone seems to look, well, really happy.

The North Downs also mark the start of London (if you call Croydon London), and stop the capital from spreading any further south for the moment, despite the odd call to start building on the green belt. From the North Downs onwards then it's goodbye to open countryside and hello to continuous urban development all the way to Victoria.

Roads to Nowhere

The train may pretty much immediately run into urban development, but the green fingers of the North Downs penetrate surprisingly far inside the M25. To the east of the line lies the Farthing Downs where amongst the peaceful green fields and mooing cows you could almost imagine you're on top of a hill in the Cotswolds, rather than on the edge of one of the biggest cities in the world (although the high rises of Croydon lying in the haze on the horizon might give the game away). You can't see any of this from the train though, as it zooms through those long cuttings before bursting out next to the Coulsdon bypass. The bypass opened in 2006 and was almost instantly nose to tail with traffic. When the train speeds past during rush hour there's an almost palpable air of smugness in the carriage, that is until the train makes one of its irregular lengthy stops just outside of East Croydon.

Driving up through south London is of course tediously slow. If you've ever had the joy of driving up the M23 into South London you might notice that the junction marking the northern end of the motorway just south of Coulsdon is actually junction 7, rather a strange number on which to start a motorway. Seen from the air the reason for this quickly becomes apparent; at the junction traffic leaves the motorway on slip roads, leaving an empty motorway to fly over junction 7 on a bridge that looks like it has real purpose ... before conking out in the middle of a field. The motorway was never finished, nor is it ever likely to be. The M3 does much the same thing, meaning that driving into London from the south is pretty nightmarish, and the drive from London to Brighton can be one hell of a slog on a hot summer's day.

If the Victorian era was the heyday for railway building then the 60s and 70s were the golden age for motorways, with three lane highways spreading like tendrils up and down the length of Britain giving us personal mobility undreamed of in times gone by. The big issue with motorways though has always been what to do with all of the traffic once it gets to the towns and cities they link; motorways move huge volumes of vehicles and if they're just dumped onto unimproved local roads the result is gridlock. The solution in the concrete loving 60s was urban motorways; traffic would arrive from the inter-city roads and travel through a network of flyovers and tunnels, before coming to a rest in massive new multi-story carparks. All around the country construction started on many of these schemes; in London the M1 and M4 penetrate deep into the city to link up with the North Circular, which was upgraded to almost motorway standard at the same time. Glasgow uniquely kept building its urban motorway network into the modern era, completing what will probably be the final link a couple of years back.

There are of course a few problems with this approach. Firstly, and probably most importantly, is the monumental cost. The pathway for a new urban road is rarely clear and homes, offices and parks need to be bought up at great expense and bulldozed. Secondly, people living near to the new roads don't normally welcome an ugly new road full of fume belching vehicles with open arms; call them NIMBYS if you like but most of us wouldn't like a new road built past our homes either. Finally the idea of filling cities full of dirty, noisy streams of traffic is thought by some people to be a little unwise to say the least; cars and people often don't make the best of neighbours. All this meant that after the 70s the general concept of the urban motorway as an all-round good idea died a death in the UK, with the honourable exception of the previously mentioned Glasgow.

Right, back to the M23, and even back in the 60s the powers that be couldn't help notice that getting out of London and down to Brighton was a bit of a long winded experience, with the main route being the single carriageway A23 that crawled through the centres of Croydon, Redhill and Crawley on the trip down to the coast. The idea of a motorway to speed traffic down to the south coast was born, but the problem remained of what to do with the traffic coming back into London. Luckily the M23 formed part of a grand masterplan for London that would have turned the capital into one of the most car friendly cities in the world or a hellish motorised nightmare, depending on your point of view.

The plan was to build four concentric orbital motorways, or Ringways, through London. Ringways 3 and 4 would form a kind of inner and outer M25, Ringway 2 would replace the north and south circular whilst Ringway 1 would place a concrete girdle round central

London, linking up with deep penetrating extensions to the M1 and M4. The M23 would connect up with this masterplan, starting at Crawley and pushing up through Croydon and Streatham to connect with Ringway 2.

Of course you don't need to be a driver to know that very little of this ever got built. Objections to the plans came thick and fast, the astronomical cost being a major one. The social objections were perhaps even stronger though; the plans would have meant the demolition of tens of thousands of homes and left over a million Londoners living within 200 meters of a motorway. Even the London Boroughs, who you might have thought would support the economic benefits that road building is claimed to bring, took a rather dim view of bulldozers driving concrete nooses through their neighbourhoods. The plans struggled on into the 70s in various mutations before the Government finally pulled funding in 1973, causing the Ringways project to collapse into the dust.

Without Ringway 2 to receive all of its traffic plans for the M23 remained on ice until the early 70s when the Department for Transport got fed up with twiddling their thumbs and decided to make a start on the southern end, linking up with the section of the M25 under construction to the south of London. The road opened in stages between 1972 and 1975, however even at this point the Government still hoped to push the motorway into London, as proved by Junction 7 with its proverbial road to nowhere still patiently waiting to be driven through the housing estates of south London. The land bought up by the Government to build the road wasn't released until the mid-90s, and from the air you can still trace some of the line into London that the road would have taken. Interestingly there don't ever seem to have been any plans to continue the motorway down to Brighton; it probably doesn't need it as the A23 is a pretty big road anyway, but it does leave Brighton with the status of the UK's largest city without a direct motorway link.

Some parts of the Ringways project did go ahead though, the most obvious example being the M25 which is a kind of bastard child of Ringways 3 and 4. The M25 was opened in 1986 after being constructed in discrete little stages over the previous decade. Plans for the motorway were never actually presented as a whole; each section was justified on its own merits and there was never a public discussion over the merits of a London orbital motorway. This is probably the legacy of the collapsed Ringways project muddying the water rather than a grand conspiracy by the road builders, however it does make you think when you hear some of the modern day calls for an 'outer' M25 as some of the new roads being built around the home counties could conceivably be linked up to provide this humongous new motorway.

Other work that went ahead included an upgrade of the north circular to its current multi-lane status in preparation for Ringway 2, however the work on the south circular never started leaving it still prone to enormous jams today (then again the north circular isn't much better). Some parts of Ringway 1 and its link roads were also built, perhaps giving an impression of what many parts of London would have looked like if the plan for motorway madness went ahead. The best example is probably the Westway road linking Paddington and Shepherds Bush – a big, ugly concrete flyover with traffic skimming along at roof height. Not very nice to live around then. It's a recurring theme of the period really; planners focusing on their narrow objectives, in this case to move cars about quickly, and failing to realise that they were turning cities into concrete crudholes.

The problem with building new roads of course is that people tend to use them – how dare they! Commuting is probably the best example; the time people spend commuting to work has actually varied remarkably little over the past few centuries. Before cars and trains gave people motorised means to get to work we all walked or rode a bike. Choice of where to live was constrained to within a few miles of work, however once mass car ownership caught on after the war people started moving much further from their work. Better roads push this process further; if a new motorway gives people the option of living somewhere that's a lot nicer, or just cheaper, they'll usually take it. This means that any relief from congestion that a new road produces is normally short lived, as it soon fills to bursting with new cars. Whisper it quietly but this is also the case with public transport, and if any of the plans to build high speed rail links currently being touted around actually come to anything we'll probably see further expansion of the London commuting circle.

The railway of course never had any need for a bulldozer, as when it was constructed this area of south London was just a widely spaced collection of small towns and villages. In fact it's a real testament to the sheer scale of house building in the 1920s and 30s that the M23 ran into so many problems. Whilst you can appreciate this from the train it's only really when you travel in on a slower form of transport that it strikes you just how many houses were built in this period, with mile upon mile of 30s style semis stretching from Couldson all of the way up to Tooting. As soldiers returned from the First World War the politicians promised 'homes fit for heroes', and after some post war struggling the construction industry revved up and started to deliver. Across the country 5 million new homes were built in this period, a staggering 25% of today's housing stock. These were, in the main, nice houses too; sturdily built with big rooms, bay windows and spacious gardens. In short they knock many of today's cramped, bathroom heavy efforts into a cocked hat, and it's no surprise that 30s houses often attract a premium from eager buyers.

The explosion in house building created many of the London suburbs we have today, which fed off the new surface rail and tube lines that let people speed from their homes in the suburbs to jobs in the city centre. This was a great period for home ownership too, with a growth in building societies allowing families to secure a mortgage on one of these new build homes for the very first time. Unfortunately the Second World War called time on this era for housing, and after the country emerged from war battered, weary and broke the priority for housing was for it to be cheap and easy, leading to the 'if it's grey and ugly let's build it' era of the 60s and 70s.

The war also led to the destruction and damage of a fair portion of London's housing stock. Hitler even had a pop at poor old Coulsdon by chucking a few V1 flying bombs at it. They didn't cause that much damage though, which is lucky as Coulsdon is actually rather pretty with lots of those 30s houses plonked down between the trees, almost as if a forest and a housing estate has suffered a bizarre time and space displacement in a mad scientist's lab. You can appreciate this view as the train makes it way up the wide valley through Coulsdon and Purley, which might take your mind off the fact that the rear half of the Brighton express derailed here in 1910, smashing into the platform at Coulsdon North and sending seven passengers to their graves.

The high rises of Croydon signal goodbye to 30s suburbia, at least temporarily, and hello to modern Britain. If modern Britain is like the Croydon Law Courts, the first building that catches the eye as the train rolls towards the station, I think most of us would hack it back into the 30s. This building was seemingly designed to make people passing through the doors think that they're already in prison, and if the Luftwaffe ever find any old flying bombs at the back of a warehouse you'd hope they'd drop one on here.

Unfortunately the courthouse isn't the only concrete monolith in Croydon; the town centre was comprehensively redeveloped in the 60s and, as par for the course during this era, they made a bit of a mess of it. Nasty concrete buildings and wide, busy roads predominate, with a cluster of poorly designed high rises chucked in for good measure. This is a shame as the place has got a lot going for it jobs wise; they boast that Croydon is London's third biggest business district after the City and Docklands.

It's probably achieved this status by being fearsomely well connected. Trains from East Croydon run all over London and the South East, and when you get outside of the station you find something rather rare in the South East: trams. Trams and trolleybuses used to be common in many towns across the UK but as the 20th century progressed most towns tore the lines out, which depending on who you talk to was either because they were old and inflexible, or part of a sinister project by the oil and vehicle industries to flog lots of cars and buses. Despite being popular all across Europe then trams in Britain were relegated to a small number of northern cities.

This is a shame, as trams are great. They're clean, quiet and quick, and above all they don't seem to suffer from the stigma attached to buses. Londoners might be shocked at this, but in most places outside of the capital you can be seen as a bit of a failure if you travel by bus, a stigma reinforced by that sourpuss Maggie Thatcher who once said that people on buses after the age of 25 were all a bunch of hopeless losers ... or something like that. Unfortunately stigmas like this tend to be self-reinforcing, and buses often become the sole preserve of the young, old, poor and truly desperate.

Despite this the Department for Transport takes a bit of a dim view of tram schemes, citing cost reasons for treating most funding proposals with a flat 'No – and by the way get a car you looser'. It's quite surprising then that Croydon became centre of a new tram system in 2000, linking Wimbledon in the west with Beckinham in the east. They probably got the money because of the state of the Tube in south London, rather like a grumpy London cabbie it doesn't really go south of the river. The tram is sort of Croydon's Tube then, and judging by the number of people using the system it seems to be rather successful.

Looking at the plans for Croydon they're going to need all of the transport links they can get, as there's work under way to 'rectify' the mistakes of the 60s with some major new redevelopment. I say 'rectify' as most of the plans on the drawing board seem to involving building a long way upwards, which unless they're done sensitively would seem to repeat rather than rectify. The first part of all of this is the Croydon Gateway scheme to the east of the station, now under construction under the more earthy title of Ruskin Square. This will be the usual mish-mash of glass and steel offices alongside small flats for commuters. The Council say that the redevelopment plans will make Croydon a hub of 'living, retailing, culture and business' by 2020. My local chum says that Croydon culture at the moment mainly involves people bottling each other on the high street on Saturday nights, so perhaps we shouldn't be too cynical if the only way is up.

East Croydon marks the point where the Thameslink trains diverge from the main line to Victoria, travelling up the original route of the railway to London Bridge before pushing on to Hertfordshire and Bedfordshire beyond. This makes it a good place to talk about the upgrade to the Thameslink line, announced recently by a great raft of posters and leaflets landing at stations. 'Blimey you kool kats', they say, 'there's some big changes to the Thameslink coming your way now, so listen up'. In plain English this means 'Think the train service sucks at the moment, we'll we're going to be right royally screwing it for the next 5 years, you can try getting on the train if you like, but quite frankly you're better off using a spacehopper'.

Do you remember a few years back when marketing departments were giving their otherwise dull products the suffix '2000' to make them sound cool and sophisticated, i.e. 'The new Crudcon Toastmaster 2000: now with MICROCHIP control for optimum browning performance!'? Now of course we know that the 21st century is exactly like the last one only with Facebook and better mobile phones; the railway industry would have probably liked to have known this in the 90s when they committed one of the cardinal errors of infrastructure projects. Never, ever, ever put a date in the title of your project, as you'll only look like a total numpty when the completion date inevitably slips. Welcome then to the Thameslink 2000 project, which quietly lost the increasingly inaccurate 2000 part of its name a couple of years ago.

The Thameslink route has existed since Victorian times, but the cross London section was closed to passenger trains for over 70 years. In 1988 some bright spark at British Rail realised that by opening up a tunnel near Holborn trains could pass straight through London, allowing passengers from the north and south to reach many destinations in London without having to use the tube. The resulting cheap ad-hoc route has bottleneck and capacity issues though, which quickly started to bite as the route proved wildly popular with the travelling public. It wasn't long then before talk started of an upgrade to the route, and Thameslink 2000 was born. That's when the problems started; recession, rail privatisation and Government wrangling sought to delay the scheme for over a decade, and it was 2007 before it was given the green light to proceed with work hopefully complete by 2015.

Finding out what the Thameslink programme actually is can prove slightly problematic, as Network Rail seem to have spent all of their money on marketing consultants who like bright colours and language that's down with the krazy kids rather than actually explaining what they're doing to the line. In essence though it's pretty simple; the project will let the line carry longer 12 carriage trains and remove bottlenecks through central London to allow lots more trains to ply routes to a wider variety of destinations. Of course that sounds simple, but in reality it means major works at many of the stations on the route and the construction of overpasses, underpasses and viaducts in central London. For an example take a peek at Blackfriars station, which is currently a gargantuan construction site as they extend the platforms and make other improvements to the station. All-in-all the project is estimated to come in at a wallet busting £5.5 billion. The upgrade doesn't mean that the trains will be any quicker, although it does mean that the horrible trains used on the route will be consigned to the knacker's yard and a new fleet of Electrostars (the same as on the Brighton to Victoria route) will be brought into replace them, with a bit more space to rest one's derrière than their predecessors.

The only cloud on the horizon as I type is the dire state of the public finances. With two major cross London train projects currently on the go, and demand for rail travel dropping during the economic downturn, you can only hope the Government puts the long term interest of the capital's infrastructure ahead of the need to claw back cash to reduce ballooning Government borrowing. Crossrail incidentally is Thameslink's east-west cousin, linking up with the Thameslink route at Farringdon. When it opens in 2018 you'll be able to get from the south coast to destinations on all points of the compass without using the tube at all. That is, of course, if it all gets built. If it follows the example set by many of Britain's transport projects in recent years it'll probably just peter out in a building site somewhere just to the west of Hammersmith.

CAPITAL APPRECIATION

After East Croydon, London proper seems to start. Before that the big gardens and trees mean you could almost imagine you're in some regional town rather than on the edge of a mega-city. London begins to show its diversity, with every skin colour and culture seemingly on display, whilst mosques by the side of the line remind you that the overwhelmingly white Christian society that built the south London suburbs in the 1930s is morphing into something far more diverse and interesting. London also does something that I've never been able to get my head round; nice areas and rough areas existing very much cheek by jowl, meaning that if you're travelling through an unfamiliar area you sometimes don't know whether people want to mug you or offer you a latte.

As the train travels up through Thornton Heath South London's biggest landmark soon heaves into view to the east of the line. Some call it London's Eiffel Tower, but this is bestowing a bit of a grand status on what's actually just a great big TV transmitter. The transmitter at Crystal Palace is London's second tallest structure though and, accompanied by its slightly stumpier twin at Croydon, it provides half of London with their daily fix of Big Brother and Britain's Wildest Car Chases.

The transmitter lies on the former site of the Crystal Palace, a huge structure of iron and glass that was the Millennium Dome of its day in more ways than one. The Palace originally sat in Hyde Park as the centrepiece of the Great Exhibition of 1851, taking a crack team of builders just nine months to construct (about the time you'd need for the site Risk Assessment these days). After the Exhibition it was moved at enormous expense to its final resting place in South London, but stuck out here the Palace never really stacked up financially as a visitor's attraction and the owners must have breathed a sigh of relief when it burnt to the ground in 1936.

Despite its long and painful decline the Palace's original role hosting the Great Exhibition was really rather special. Planned by Queen Victoria's big squeeze, Prince Albert, the Exhibition showed off the brightest, biggest and best of British technology as the country revelled in its status as the workshop of the world. Visitors were able to gaze in wonder at exhibits that included an early version of the fax machine and the world's biggest diamond, before being entertained by the first national motor show, dog shows and an aeronautical exhibition. They could also relieve themselves in the world's first public toilets, whose charges led to the phrase 'spending a penny', which of course could do with being updated to 'spending 30p' judging by the current charges in Victoria station.

Six million people visited the Great Exhibition. It made so much money that the profits paid for the establishment of the grand museums of Knightsbridge that are so synonymous with London today. So many people were present at any one time that some feared revolutionary fervour might break out in the assembled throngs of proles, no doubt driven by the desire to snaffle the world's largest diamond. This of course didn't happen, and, coming back to the modern world, the most likely situation that would now ever see an angry mob descend onto the streets of London would be a failure of the Crystal Palace transmitter depriving people of the weekly dose of the X-Factor. Actually, that's probably a bit mean on the residents of south London; apparently a province in India is trying to get more televisions installed to bring down the birth rate, so perhaps the real outcome of the transmitter falling over in a storm would be a mini baby boom 9 months later.

This section of the line into central London was just about the only part where the railway builders had the headache of urban development to contend with; further south the railway pretty much created the towns and cities it passes through, and the line could just be ploughed through open countryside. As a result the line starts to twist and weave as it gets closer and closer to central London, following the line of least resistance where the railway company wouldn't have to demolish too many houses. One result is that the line does something that would be completely flabbergasting to the modern mind: it makes a bee line for London's green spaces.

London's parks and commons make it a surprisingly green city, and for many people access to these green spaces makes the difference between urban life being enjoyable or an endless drudgery. On a sunny day the commons of south London are packed full of people having picnics, kicking a ball about or just sitting down and enjoying the peace and quiet. So if a few chaps in hard hats rolled up one day and told everyone to bugger off as they were building a massive great railway smack through the middle we'd probably see protests that made the 90s anti road building movement look like a teddy bear's picnic. However, in the early 19th century this is precisely what happened, and the line skirts the edge of Norbury Park before slashing straight across Tooting Bec and Wandsworth Commons. Despite being unceremoniously cut in two the Commons are still nice places to spend a sunny afternoon, with huge grassy fields just aching for a ball to be booted around sitting alongside the odd lake, tennis court, bowling green and even a pub or two.

As the train belts across Tooting Bec Common you might catch a glimpse of the lido, or perhaps not as the designers tried to hide it from view of both the rail line and the Common itself presumably in case a gentleman caught sight of a lady in her swimming cossie. Lidos, in case you're not familiar with them, are simply open air swimming pools. Tooting Bec is the granddaddy of them all; it's both the largest and one of the first to be constructed (1906). Actually it's still the largest fresh water swimming pool in the country, and makes an Olympic sized swimming pool look positively tiddly by comparison. Lidos really took off in the 1930s – at Tooting I'm guessing this was probably due to mixed bathing being introduced in 1931 – and then fell out of favour in modern times due to cheap foreign holidays and local authorities baulking at the costs of keeping them open. Luckily Tooting Bec was preserved, giving the local kids somewhere to hang out on those hot summer days, and providing eagle eyed train passengers the opportunity to glimpse the odd bathing beauty or basking hunk.

After the commons fade away the train is very much in the heart of the Victorian city; no more 1930s suburbs, just row after row of Victorian terraces showing their often shabby rears to the train as it trundles on to Clapham Junction. Clapham marks the point where trains from the Southern network travelling to Victoria cross the path of South West Trains travelling to Waterloo, allowing Clapham Junction to proudly display 'Britain's Busiest Railway Station!' on its sign. This is a bit difficult to comprehend; OK, it's busy but it's not full of a million grumpy suited and booted commuters charging around like Waterloo station at rush hour. But more importantly why is being 'busiest' a thing you want to be advertised? Being Britain's busiest station means more likelihood of congestion, delays and having to push through London's hordes in order to change trains. Maybe we should celebrate this though, and other top ranked facilities in our fair isles could follow Clapham Junction's lead. How about, 'Selefield – Britain's Most Radioactive Nuclear Power Station!' or 'Heathrow Airport – Britain's Noisiest Neighbour!'.

Anyway, it turns out that the 'busiest' in this case refers to the number of trains passing through, which explains the number of train-spotters hanging round at the end of platform 12. Now train-spotters have a bad rap, it's really just another form of the male obsessiveness that grips most of us blokes at some point in our lives. The difference is that if you're, say, obsessed with playing guitar you form a band, your mates think your cool and girls want to have sex with you. If you're obsessed with trains though people generally think you're a sado, and the only female that's interested in you is your Gran. Train-spotting must have been a lot more interesting in the days of steam when trains weren't built to identical designs and roared past in exciting clouds of cinders and steam. These days though it must be hard to get excited about a constant stream of identical Electrostars humming through on their silent electric motors.

Train-spotters were mourning the loss of some of their beloved trains in 1988; although more seriously a lot of people were mourning the loss of their loved ones, as the 12th December of that year saw the worst train crash of modern times. The crash took place just south of Clapham Junction, with signalling cock ups causing a commuter train travelling in from Poole to run into the back of another packed train stopped at a signal. To add insult to injury the wreckage was then hit by an empty train running out of Clapham Junction, killing several survivors of the original crash. In all 35 people died and nearly 500 were injured; many more would have died if not for the prompt actions of the emergency services and the pupils of a nearby school who rushed to help at the scene.

If you're on the train as you read this I hope you're sitting comfortably. Crashes have been a mercifully rare occurrence on the London to Brighton line, but like any long-in-the-tooth line incidents have stacked up over the last 170 years. Whilst accidents are always going to happen, the question is are we doing all we can to minimise them now? The investigation into the Clapham crash suggested two areas for improvement; firstly the trains themselves weren't particularly crash-worthy, and secondly automatic systems that stop trains from passing red signals, common in many other countries, really should be installed. The crash-worthiness problem with the old slam door trains stemmed from their 50s style design and construction. The carriages were built with a strong, heavy chassis (lower part with the wheels and other mechanical gubbins), whilst the actual carriage bodies themselves were relatively light and flimsy. In a low speed collision this system worked; the big heavy bits hit end to end with a loud 'thunk' and everybody walked off shaken up but unharmed. Unfortunately in a faster crash the heavy chassis of one train tended to jump up and plough through the lightweight carriagework of the other, with deadly consequences for their occupants. The process of phasing out these trains was slow, but now all the trains operating in the South East are of more crash-worthy modern designs.

The introduction of automatic train stopping systems has been less successful though. I'm willing to bet that most car drivers have inadvertently run a red light from time to time – you're tired, distracted or the sun is in your eyes. But most of the time if there's actually anything coming you see the danger and manage to stop in time. Unfortunately similar things happen with train drivers, indeed inquiries into train disasters often reveal just how common incidents of trains passing red signals actually are. But when the driver spots danger ahead it's almost impossible to stop an enormously heavy train in time to avoid a smash. The solution the Clapham inquiry recommended was to fit funky automatic systems that calculated the speed of the train and the position of any red lights; if the driver doesn't stop they give him a warning then apply the brakes before the train can pass through the red signal. This is all quite expensive though, and the Conservative Government of the time was far more interested in privatising the network to make a quick buck rather than shelling out for pricey safety systems. The compromise introduced was a radio beacon system that tells a train when it has passed, or is about to pass, a red signal. Whilst this is better than nothing it can't avert disaster in cases of rear end collisions, or where a train is travelling faster than 75 mph. Something to think about when the train is travelling at 90 mph on the longer stretches of line.

A RIGHT ROYAL ENDING

Clapham usually sees the train leave the station groaning with passengers, and, laden with its heavy human cargo, it picks its way slowly into Battersea. This is known for three things, namely the park, power station and dog's home. I won't say much about the dog's home; suffice to say that judging from the amount of barking emanating from it there's a fair few occupants. You won't hear that from the train, but you can't miss Battersea Power Station with its art deco design and four imposing towers recognisable from the Pink Floyd 'Animals' album cover (although without the inflatable pig in the real world). The station was a big coal burning job built in the 1930s and extended in the 50s. Power stations in cities are a bit of an oddity now, they tend to be built in the back of beyond with the pylons of the national grid fizzling and crackling as they shift electricity round the country to where it's needed. Back in the day though urban power stations made perfect sense; with no grid to work with you built the power stations where the demand was. There's a spin off benefit with this too; power stations produce vast amounts of waste heat, and in town this can be used to provide heating and hot water for surrounding homes rather than just dumping it in seas and rivers. As Pimlico was redeveloped after the war its residents were therefore able to benefit from heating provided by their giant neighbour across the river.

One of the big issues that made urban power stations fall out of favour was pollution; burning vast quantities of coal produces equally vast quantities of air pollution. Even in the 30s this was something of a worry, although concerns around the time Battersea was constructed tended to focus on the potential effects of pollution on the paintings in the Tate gallery across the river rather than the more mundane ability of coal smoke to kill Londoners. It took another twenty years and a seminal pollution event for the Government to start taking the issue more seriously. During the Great Smog of 1952 coal smoke from houses and factories got so bad that people were getting lost in the street and theatres had to be shut as the audience couldn't see the stage. Oh, and thousands of people were shuffled off to their graves. The partial solution at Battersea was to install a water scrubbing system to get the nastier stuff out of the chimney emissions. Unfortunately all of the rubbish had to go somewhere, and in this case that somewhere was the River Thames. As you might imagine this didn't have a particularly great effect on the fish, and the scrubbers were eventually turned off in the 60s.

Battersea finally closed for good in 1983 and since then battles have raged over what to do with the site, with everything from raising it to the ground to converting it into a rival for the Millennium Dome being mooted. The station itself looks a little sickly these days with the smashed windows and scaffolding-a-plenty that's visible from the train line giving the impression that the place is probably held together with lollipop sticks and gaffer tape. The current proposal is for a mixed development of housing, shops, hotels and offices that would keep the original power station building and provide it with a new companion in the form of a glistening glass and steel skyscraper. This forms part of plans for redevelopment of this area of London as a whole that would include extending the Northern Line down to Battersea to provide a fast link to the rest of the city.

Interestingly the plans also include restarting power generation at Battersea by installing a plant burning wood and general waste. This falls in with a bit of a trend at the moment to bring power generation back into towns and cities, with small power stations burning wood and other renewable fuels. The driver is of course climate change; burning wood generally has lower emissions of the greenhouse gas carbon dioxide than conventional fuels such as coal, oil or gas, especially if the waste heat can be used in surrounding flats and offices. You do, however, get the impression that the policy makers driving these changes have goldfish like memories, and are forgetting the lessons of the London smogs. Whilst modern wood burning kit is undoubtedly cleaner than the coal fires of old it's still far more polluting than the gas boilers and far off power stations that most of us rely on today to heat and power our homes. And rather than spewing out of chimneys in far off remote locations the pollution from these modern urban stations is emitted directly into the areas where we all live and work. You can only hope that those in charge see the light and strike a balance between climate protection and pollution control, as despite the closure of Battersea and its siblings London's zillion cars and buses make the air in the capital pretty yucky to start with, as anyone who's suffered black bogey syndrome will attest.

Hopefully any pollution from the new little power station won't affect Battersea Park as it's another one of London's green jewels. In fact it's one of London's better green jewels, and although smaller than its more famous neighbours north of the river it's littered with things to stare at and interesting nooks and crannies. The park was originally a site called Battersea Fields, which was a popular place for the nobility to take pot shots at each other when they felt their honour had been insulted. It's interesting to note the change in attitude to shooting people. In bygone days if you felt someone had given you insufficient respect you went down to Battersea Fields and shot them. As a result you were given a knighthood. These days if you feel someone has disrespected you and shoot them you get locked up for life and make the front page of the Daily Mail.

That's more than a little flippant; duelling in those days was covered by a 26 point code of conduct that aimed to resolve the dispute before hot lead became the only recourse, as well as laying down how the duel itself should be fought. Duelling pistols were of the single shot variety, and both parties would have an equal chance to shoot the other rather than being peppered in the back by a spray of bullets from an automatic weapon. That said, duelling was still frowned upon in the eyes of the law, and one of the advantages of Battersea Fields was its position on the edge of town; handy if you happened to win your duel and needed to make a hasty exit to the country to avoid the cops. The grey position of duelling in the eyes of the law makes it all the more surprising that the most famous duel fought at Battersea happened to involve the sitting Prime Minister of the United Kingdom.

The PM in question was the Iron Duke himself: Arthur Wellesley the Duke of Wellington. After whupping the French at Trafalgar he'd taken up a career in politics, and eventually became Prime Minister in 1828. Unbelievably in these relatively recent times Irish Catholics were still second class citizens in the eyes of the law, and couldn't, for example, sit in Parliament even if they were elected as an MP. Faced with a potential civil war in Ireland Wellington reluctantly started to push through reforms to allow the Irish Catholics greater freedom; however his political opponents strongly attacked his proposals and one, the Earl of Winchilsea, got a bit personal. Wellington felt there was only one way to proceed: shoot the bastard.

On the morning of Saturday 21st March 1829 the two met at Battersea Fields to sort out their differences, accompanied by their seconds (chums) and a doctor in case the worst happened. Despite his military background Wellington was a notoriously bad shot, and as the crunch point finally came he must have been mightily relieved to see Winchilsea keep his gun down - at the last minute he'd decided that shooting the PM might not be the best of ideas. Wellington returned the favour by firing wide of the now defenceless Winchilsea. Or just missing – accounts differ! Honour suitably regained Winchilsea apologised for his remarks, Wellington accepted and the Irish Catholics were subsequently given their freedom. All in all an interesting point in British political history; perhaps modern politicians might be dissuaded from making some of their more personal attacks if they thought their opponents on the other benches might make a pistol gesture and point towards Battersea.

But Battersea is no longer such an easy place to have a good, clean fight, as it was converted into a park in the 1850s with little bits and pieces of interest being added to it ever since. The biggest additions to the park formed part of the Festival of Britain in 1951; this was Britain's 'we're skint, our economy's on the ropes but let's have a party anyway' moment, who knows maybe the idea is due a comeback in these modern financially stressed days. The Festival saw the park gain a fun fair and a sprawling water garden. The fountains and pools of the water gardens are still with us, giving something for the young and young at heart to splash through on a hot day. The fun fair has gone though; its wooden roller-coaster derailed in 1972 and killed five children, which led to the decline and eventual removal of all of the attractions.

A more modern addition is the glitzy Peace Pagoda built on the banks of the Thames, construction of which formed the last act of Ken Livingstone's first reign as London head honcho before the Greater London Authority was temporarily abolished by Margaret Thatcher. The combination of green space, river, formal gardens, fountains and oddities make the park a popular place to visit, and on a summer's day the park teems with families out cycling and roller-skating, kids running through the fountains and students seemingly happy to sit under a tree and self-consciously ponder the meaning of life. Like most of London's green spaces Battersea Park seems to bring a little colour into everyday Londoners' otherwise grey and noisy urban lives.

One last physical barrier remains before the railway finally hits the buffers at Victoria, namely the River Thames. Compared to the tunnels and viaducts on the line further south throwing the Grosvenor Bridge over the river must have been a comparatively easy step. It's notable though that this was the first ever railway crossing of the Thames, nobody before thinking that a north-south railway might be a good idea. It's an unfortunate symptom of the fragmented way in which the British railway system developed that each railway company built their own terminal in London, with nobody really thinking that a bit of co-operation might be in order so that people travelling across the city could just switch trains at a big central station rather than be forced to hack across town by tube or bus (or, back in the day, horse and carriage) to change trains. It's only now that this situation is being belatedly rectified by projects such as Thameslink and Crossrail, which should remove some of the harried looking passengers making the journey round the Circle Line with umpteen suitcases.

Grosvenor Bridge is now of course far from the only railway crossing of the Thames; as the Thames cuts a swathe through the heart of Southern England it's festooned with crossing points: 214 bridges, over 20 tunnels, 6 public ferries and a solitary ford. If you've got a week or two to spare you can follow the river from source to sea by walking the 180 odd miles of the Thames Path, which, as the name suggests, starts where the river dribbles out from under a stone in Gloucestershire and ends at the enormous gates of the Thames Barrier. At the start of the river all it needs is a drainpipe to get it under the ancient Fosse Way road, but by the time it reaches the eastern side of the M25 the half mile long QE2 Bridge is needed to do the job.

The Thames and London have a bit of a love-hate relationship. Whilst the river historically provided water to the city and carried away its waste it also had the occasional nasty habit of flooding the city. Rather than water pouring down from the rainy hills to the west though the main threat comes from the North Sea. Out here storms can act somewhat like a giant version of someone blowing on a glass of water; this forms a bulge of water that travels down the North Sea and funnels up the Thames estuary. As the estuary narrows this storm tide rises, and the results can be catastrophic flooding. Most recently the Great Flood of 1953 killed hundred across the east of England and forced thousands more from their homes.

The solution to this problem is the Thames Barrier, which is designed to stop these floods in their tracks by physically blocking the rising water from entering the city. Why it doesn't just go round is still a mystery to me; it's probably frightened of Cockneys. Since opening with great fanfare in 1983 the barrier has been quietly defending London from floods by closing its huge gates a couple of times a year. Recently though it's been more than a couple; the barrier is designed to protect the city against a one in a hundred year flood, but in recent years the frequency of potential flood events has increased and the fear is that with climate change causing sea levels to rise the barrier may prove to be inadequate for the task sooner rather than later.

Once safely on the northern banks it's a short hop for the train into Victoria and the end of the line. Victoria solved a bit of a problem for the London, Brighton and South Coast Railway company when it opened in 1860, namely that most of the Londoners who wanted to travel down to Brighton lived north of the river whilst all of the railway's stations lay to the south, meaning passengers had to trek across the river (no tube in those days) to catch the train. The solution was to construct a station closer to Westminster and the fashionable West End, and Victoria was born. Originally it was two separate stations, one to serve the Brighton main line and the other for trains travelling out to Kent. The two were linked in a Property Ladder style knock through in 1924, however the division is still pretty obvious with each side of the station having a significantly different architectural style inside and out.

Modern Victoria is one of London's middling stations; whilst it lacks the grandeur of the recently reopened St. Pancras it's not cramped and stuffy like Kings Cross. Once you've twiddled your thumbs waiting for the guard to scratch his bum and open the doors the hustle and bustle of London is upon you. The station concourse seems to permanently thrum with the entire spectrum of travelling humanity, whilst the crush for the tube station can get so bad that a sliding cattle gate is often deployed to stop any more people from packing into the tunnels.

Outside cars, taxis and endless streams of big red buses spill their human contents into the station. Early pictures of the station show a similar scene nearly 150 years ago, with the difference being the big red buses are replaced by black and white horses and carts. We often think pollution and safety issues arose in the modern age, with the exhaust emissions of a bus likely to get you if the front end doesn't hit you first. Back in the day though they must have had problems with phenomenal quantities of disease ridden horse manure being dropped on the streets of London, and probably the odd spooked horse panicking through the streets. Same shit, different century so to speak.

The station perhaps perfectly encapsulates the era in which it was built. On one hand we have its name; Victoria, good old Queen Vic, sat on her throne dressed in black and in a permanent sulk after the loss of her beloved Albert. We take the mick out the Victorians these days, often painting them as uptight repressed types who covered up their table legs in case they found them a turn on. On the other hand we have the engineering genius behind the railway lines reaching out from the station building. Victoria's reign saw huge leaps forward in technology that saw Britain transformed from a so-so European country to the richest and most powerful nation in the world; much of what we think of as modern Britain owes a huge debt to this period of our history. Most of the icons of London hail from the Victorian days – Buckingham Palace, the Houses of Parliament, the Museums and the parks are all Victorian constructions. Our railways too nearly all date from this era, and whilst steam has given way to electricity and diesel the basic idea of transporting people and freight in carriages running on steel rails hasn't changed a jot in nearly 200 years.

And why should it? In a small country such as Britain it's difficult to think of a better way of getting large quantities of people from city to city. Much of what the London to Brighton railway passes through has changed radically in the line's near 170 year history; cities and towns have massively expanded, motorways and trunk roads have been constructed and airports have grown like enormous concrete moulds. The railway meanwhile continues to run past using its original trackbeds, bridges and tunnels.

In 170 year's time who knows how we'll be getting about; maybe the flying cars we were promised in the 1950s will have come about and the motorways crumbled to dust, whilst Gatwick will be hosting space planes to fly us round the world in minutes rather than hours. I'd hazard a bet though that the railway will still be there with slightly funkier trains, a few minutes off the journey times and hopefully better excuses than leaves on the line when the train inexplicable grinds to a halt.

Hitting the Buffers

A journey on the London to Brighton line is a pretty mundane part of many people's lives; a daily commute for thousands, and the quiet before the sensory storm of seaside fun for people coming the other way. But two things strike me as I finish off this book. The first is a profound respect for the people who built the line; they didn't have the computer aided design and earth moving equipment that we enjoy now, just the engineering genius of the Victorian age and a whole lot of manpower. Despite this they built nearly 50 miles of track with all of the bridges and tunnels it needed in less than four years, a feat that stands comparison to almost any civil engineering project of our modern age.

The second thing is that despite all of the people, offices, cars and planes crammed into this little corner of the country the Sussex and Surrey countryside remains really rather special. Whilst you get a sense of this whizzing through on the train it's only really when you take the journey slowly that you really take it in. Whilst researching this little book I've sat on a hill admiring the rolling scenery of the South Downs, parked up for lunch by streams in the High Weald and zoomed down the North Downs on my bike towards the far off towers of Croydon beyond. There are very few places in the country where you can see a wider variety of stunning countryside in such a small area. And whilst we generally have a nasty habit of cocking up our surroundings, many of our constructions add to the scenery rather than detract; the South Downs are all the better for their windmills, whilst few would argue that the Ouse valley would look better without the majestic viaduct that carries the railway across. Even some relatively recent additions like the Ardingly reservoir add a bit of a flourish to the surrounding countryside, proving that development and the natural world can live side by side if we give it a bit of thought.

Even South London has a certain charm. For most of us it's somewhere to get through as fast as possible as we run to work, meetings or a social occasion in the city centre, and people often seem to suggest that the southern suburbs are dangerous, dull or a bit of both. But some areas are actually rather nice; big spacious 1930s houses co-existing with expansive parks and commons, where the looks on people's faces suggest that city living isn't the constant drudge that some of us outside of London tend to think it is.

Not all impressions are positive though. Many of the towns that dot the railway's route to the capital are just plain ugly and dull; Haywards Heath, Horley, Redhill and the rest all seem to lack any kind of vital spark that would give them an identity of their own, rather than simply existing as dormitories where commuters go to sleep. And rather than addressing the shortcomings of these towns the planners seem to be actively targeting their expansion, with big developments of bathrooms with a bit of living space attached, or what passes for new homes these days. Now maybe I just don't get the appeal, perhaps people don't want the hurly burly of a town like Brighton, or simply can't afford a nice little rural idyll like Balcombe. It wouldn't seem to be a huge leap of the imagination though for the planners and developers to think outside the bare bones of their brief, and start providing places to live that combine peace and affordability with a sense of community and a bit of va-va-voom.

At the end of a book that's sort of nominally about local history you'd expect to see a long list of further reading if you're interested in anything covered. I wouldn't bother though; most local history books are dreadfully boring. Brighton library has a number of books on the history of the railway if you really wanted to look at them, but be warned though that they're a little dry. Instead I'd recommend going and having a look for yourself; go for a walk on the North or South Downs, have a pint in the Half Moon in Balcombe before sleeping it off under the arches of the Ouse valley viaduct, or even ignore the warning signs and saunter round the Royal Earlsfield Asylum for Idiots like you own one of the posh looking flats. There's a train station every few miles making it easy to make a few Sunday 'food and a stroll between the stations' style trips.

If you're feeling a bit more active at 54 miles Brighton to London, or vice-versa, is a good bike ride for anyone who's moderately fit. Pick your route carefully though as the High Weald in particularly can be a right drag for your legs, with many of the roads going up and down constantly for miles on end. The route of the London to Brighton bike ride isn't a bad one, in fact the ride itself is a good day out if you're in need of motivation, but start early if you don't want to get stuck in queues that make the M25 look positively tame.

On the way up or down you might get the chance to check out things you've spotted from the train. If you've read this far I'm guessing that you're a fairly regular passenger on the London to Brighton line, and perhaps you've got your own favourite landmark that jumps out as you zip past on the train (mine is the Royal Earlsfield Asylum for Idiots if only because of the name). Sorry if I haven't covered yours, but I hope this book makes that familiar journey just a little bit more interesting.

Ed Dearnley has lived in Brighton on and off for 15 years, where he has developed a complex love-hate relationship with seagulls. He works in environmental policy for the charity Environmental Protection UK, a job which keeps him running up and down to London just enough to keep life interesting. London to Brighton Derailed is his first book.

1477624R0

Printed in Great Britain by
Amazon.co.uk, Ltd.,
Marston Gate.